The Shape of the World

[handwritten signature]

Safe Travels!

Essays on Travel, Culture, and Belief
from *Rotary* magazine

By Frank Bures

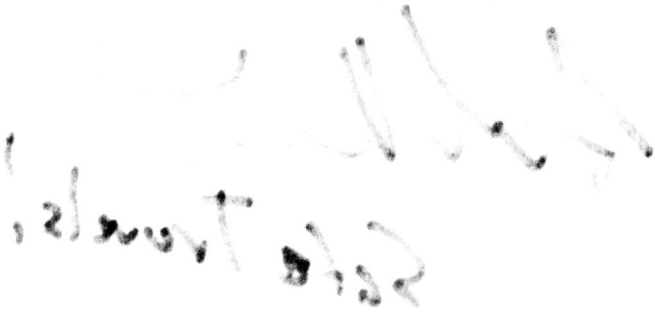

The essays in *Shape of the World* were originally published in *Rotary*.

Copyright Frank Bures

Published by Mountains Never Meet Publishing

ISBN: 9798839004696

Cover photo by Sachith Hettigodage

www.frankbures.com

For Libby and Josie,
for the laughter
for the love
and for the lessons

Contents

Belief

Stories

Rotary

Preface

In 2009, I was traveling across West Africa when I stopped in a hostel in Bamako, the capital of Mali. Inside the compound was a truck parked. On the hood of the truck there was painted a giant wheel and the words "Rotary International." When I got home from that trip, I sent an email to the general address at *The Rotarian* magazine, explaining that I'd seen the Rotary sign in Mali and suggesting if I were traveling somewhere like that again, I might offer my services in writing about clubs or projects that would be hard to reach.

A few months later, I got a response from editor Jenny Llakmani. We talked on the phone, and she suggested I write a column. We agreed on an idea, and now it appears in this book as "Sense and Sensitivity."

Over the following years, I wrote more than 50 columns for *Rotary* magazine, in addition to other many stories. It's been an adventure and a privilege to work the with the magazine's editors, and a joy to be able roam the world of ideas as widely as I was allowed.

Most of the essays collected here center around questions of culture, language, belief, the power of both travel to change the way we see the world, and the power of stories to change the way we live in it.

In some stories, I took readers on terrible truck rides through Cambodia, got scammed in Thailand, and watched the rise of "fame" as a cultural value. In all of these pieces, we saw how the inner world we create influences the outer world we live in. Along the way, I also tried to answer (or at least ask) questions like, "How do you be a good person?" "How can you cultivate wisdom?" and "What does it mean to have hope?"

The close reader will see that I am obsessed with the power of words and stories, and in many of these pieces, I explore the way language shapes our world, the power of family stories to give our life meaning, and how reading fiction makes you a better person.

The last section is specifically for Rotarians. These are columns that pertain to how to increase the impact of your club on the world and even on fellow club members.

In the end, I hope these essays give you something to think about as you navigate the currents of our fast-changing world. And I hope they provide a few more logs to shore up your raft as it drifts down the great river of stories and carries you out to sea.

Introduction

The first piece I ever read by Frank Bures was an article titled "How to Use a Squat Toilet." A colleague emailed me a link with a note that went something like, "You've got to read this!" I'd been immersing myself in all things toilet-related — I'd just edited a feature on the topic for *The Rotarian* magazine — and I was electrified by Frank's piece. It was informative, hilarious, and a bit shocking. I sent him a note.

Frank had written to us after seeing the Rotary logo painted on a truck in Mali, but if he thought it strange that *The Rotarian* magazine would respond primarily thanks to his article about the logistics of going to the loo, he never let on. It was the beginning of a beautiful friendship — between Frank and me, and between Frank and Rotarians. Although I've never counted, I'm willing to bet that over the years, his columns have received more responses from readers than any other writer's in the magazine's history.

Reading through these columns again now, I'm struck by the timelessness of his work. Even after more than 10 years in some cases, the pieces are as relevant as when they first appeared —some of them even more so.

His first column for the magazine (now called *Rotary*) appeared in August 2010. It was titled "Sense and Sensitivity," and in it, Frank talked about how there's more to translation than dictionary definitions. He wrote, "Words are like icebergs: The basic meaning is visible above the surface, but there are vast chambers of meanings below."

That description encapsulates Frank's writing, too. His pieces are always fun and interesting to read, but they are also invariably thought-provoking, with layers of meaning to ponder. Writing at the intersection of insight and information, he uses data and research to help understand the phenomena he sees in the world, but never closes the door on wonder — or even magic.

"For me," he continued in that first piece, "this is one of the great joys of traveling the world and learning different ways of thinking, of feeling, and of being: to land on some new shore of the mind, to look around and admire the view."

Over the years, Frank and I have exchanged hundreds of emails and spent hours and hours on the phone talking over column ideas. We've shared articles we think are fascinating, recommended books and movies to each other, and traded videos of our favorite '80s bands. In all that time, we've never met in person, but thanks to the journeys we've taken via these essays, in the passport of my mind, there's a country where I found laughter, insight, and a new way of seeing things. And the stamp on that page says "Frank."

--Jenny Llakmani, former Managing Editor, *Rotary* magazine

March 2022

TRAVEL

What price experience? On money and memories

It was after 17 hours — in no fewer than 10 vehicles — along a jolting, washed-out road between Thailand and Cambodia that I first appreciated some basic things about air travel. On a plane, there is no rain. There are no bags of fruit leaking unknown juices onto your backpack. There are no bruised tailbones from an entire day spent hammering over rocks and potholes. And on a plane, when you cross an international border, drinks are on the house.

I ran over this list of perks as I hung off the back of a pickup truck, watching my right foot disappear under layers of mud. My other leg was twisted underneath me, with no feeling left in it. My arms ached as I gripped a leaky plastic tarp that looked like it had been used for target practice by the Khmer Rouge. Periodically, the tarp pressed down in an inverted parachute that threatened to smother us all. Bridgit, my wife, was perched next to me, holding on to nothing but my pant leg.

Eventually we arrived in Cambodia, where our $3 room with a ceiling fan and a cold shower felt like the Ritz-Carlton on Maui. The next day, we walked around the ruins of the Angkor kingdom.

I thought about that trip recently as Bridgit and I (now with a house in Minnesota and two daughters) sat down to look at our retirement planning. If you were an investment adviser, you would have been clicking your tongue and shaking your head. Bridgit, an accountant, clicked her tongue and shook her head.

"Look," I said, trying to cheer her up, "if we'd done what everyone says you should do — if we'd gotten jobs straight out of college, kept our heads down and worked till we retired — we might have ended up like those people on the boat."

Those people on the boat were a retired couple I'd read about in the local newspaper. They'd worked hard their whole lives and were excited about their first trip overseas, a 16-day Mediterranean cruise. Two hours after setting sail, their ship — the *Costa Concordia* — hit a rock. All but 32 of the 3,229 passengers escaped. The retirees weren't among them.

That's not to say they lived their lives badly. But their story filled me with gratitude for the things we'd done. Instead of investing in a 401(k), we'd invested in memories.

"True," Bridgit said. "But that doesn't mean we don't need to get saving, unless you want to be working until you're 80."

This was a fair point. I understand the wisdom of saving, of investing and of being careful with money. But how do you strike a balance between seizing the day and saving up for it?

I came across a book called *Happy Money: The Science of Smarter Spending*, by Elizabeth Dunn, who teaches psychology at the University of British Columbia, and Michael Norton, a professor of marketing at Harvard. They explore this question scientifically.

For several centuries, classic economic theory has held that more money is better: The higher people's salaries, the happier they will be. But economists have started to realize that this isn't true. For example, they've discovered that people who earn $55,000 are not twice as happy as people who earn $25,000. They are only 9 percent happier. And once people reach $75,000 in income, more money has no impact at all.

This was the starting point for Dunn and Norton, who asked: If more money doesn't matter, what does? Among their conclusions is that "experiences" are a better value than "things." Fifty-seven percent of people said an "experiential purchase" made them happier, while only 34 percent said a material purchase did. Among Americans over age 50, only one spending category made a measurable difference in satisfaction: leisure, such as trips, movies, and sporting events. Even owning a house has no effect on overall satisfaction. And when asked to look back on past purchases, 83 percent of people said their biggest regret was passing up an experience they could have had. With material purchases, the biggest regret was buying something they later realized they didn't want.

One reason for this, Dunn and Norton write, is that "experiences are more likely to make us feel connected to others." Another is that after buying something, our satisfaction with it declines, while the opposite seems true for experiences. When researchers followed students on a three-week cycling trip replete with rain and mosquitoes and sore muscles, 61 percent of the riders reported feeling disappointed with the journey while they were on it. But afterward, only 11 percent did.

Part of this difference has to do with how purchases affect our use of time. Dunn and Norton say this should be our primary concern when we consider financial decisions: Buying a giant flat-screen TV may make you happy as you walk out of the store, but "what we are buying is an implicit commitment to plunking ourselves in front of it — often alone — for one-sixth of the next year." And in every study, people who watch more television are less satisfied with their lives than people who watch less.

This is mainly because TV takes us away from other people, according to Dunn and Norton. Social relationships are emerging as the foundation of happiness. In one study, when people received a gift certificate with instructions to spend it on either themselves or someone else, people who'd spent the money on others were measurably happier than those who hadn't. The ones who were happiest were those who bought a coffee for someone and spent time with that person.

When I pushed Bridgit to read the book, she told me I was trying to justify my purchase of a kayak. ("It's not a kayak, it's the experience of kayaking!" I said.) Maybe I was grasping at straws, trying to justify not only my kayak but my whole life. Still, I couldn't help feeling a little better about the time I'd spent out in the world. I couldn't think of a place I regretted visiting.

Even though our road trip to Cambodia was torturous and exhausting, somehow its value accrued over time. Taking a plane would have been faster. Staying home and working would have been more lucrative. But would we have remembered any of that? I knew how those cyclists felt. As the Roman philosopher Seneca said, "Things that were hard to bear are sweet to remember."

At least we have that much in the bank.

March 2014

Travelers beware: On scams

Picture, if you will, a tall man walking around Athens. He is staring at the buildings, unable to read the signs. He has only a vague idea of where he is. He has a wild mane of graying hair poking out from under his Gatsby cap, and he would never be mistaken for a Greek.

He's my father-in-law.

This was some years ago. He told us the story later: A man approached him and introduced himself. He said he'd lived in the United States and wanted to practice his English. My father-in-law said he was in a hurry, but the man insisted on buying him a drink. So he shrugged and went along to a little bar around the corner.

They talked for a few minutes. Then a couple of women joined them, and soon the man disappeared. The women were friendly — very friendly — and started ordering drinks. Then more drinks. "Boy," my father-in-law thought, "these Greeks sure are friendly." And then, "I wonder who's paying for all these drinks?" As he got up to leave, he was presented with a bill for $30.

He got his answer: The sucker was paying.

Tourism, even in its legitimate form, is an extractive industry, mining the pockets of outsiders. Often, there's a fine line between a lawful transaction and a scam. But the fact is that most of us who travel will be scammed at some point, whether it's by a money changer, a market vendor, or a mobster. They can see you coming from miles away — your clothes, your gait, the way you look around. You try to blend in. But they still find you.

Some scams are timeless, replicated in various permutations throughout the world. There is the police scam, in which someone purporting to be a police officer tries to extract a bribe for some "problem" with your passport. (Tell him to follow you to the nearest police station.) There's the rear-ending scam, in which a car in front of you slams on the brakes, then someone removes your luggage from your trunk. (Keep your bags in the car with you.) There's the bird dropping/mustard scam, in which the moment you find yourself covered with a given substance, someone mysteriously appears with a towel to clean you off — meanwhile, also cleaning out your wallet. (Keep your wits about you.)

Scams often are more of an annoyance than a real danger. They are also relatively rare. You shouldn't go around suspecting that everyone is out to steal your wallet. Kindness, generosity, and altruism are the currency of social interaction, and no society can function without them. Still, anonymity is the enemy of altruism, and the shallow relationships of travel are too much for some elements to resist.

By definition, a scam is something you don't figure out until it's happened. When my wife and I moved to Bangkok, Thailand, we fell for a scam we had actually read about.

We were walking along the wall of the royal palace when a guy came up to us. "Hello," he said. "How are you today?" His English was suspiciously polished. He asked where we were going, and we told him.

"Oh, sorry, the palace is closed today," he said. "Thai holiday! But there is another temple that is open." He flagged down a seemingly random túk-túk. As if hypnotized, we climbed on.

The túk-túk sped off and took us to a tailor shop. We went in, looked around, slightly confused, then came out. The driver wasn't happy. "OK. We go one place, then I take you to see standing Buddha." He pulled into a small alleyway filled with túk-túks bearing other *farang* (foreigners). He pointed to the door of a large gem store. We went in, looked around again, then came out.

"No, no!" he said. "You go too fast. You go back, take long time looking."

"We don't want to buy anything," I said.

"No problem," he said. "You just looking, I get free *rotang.*"

"Free what?" I asked.

He pointed to his gas tank, and I understood. We went into the shop and browsed through several floors of overpriced, possibly fake gems. When we finally came out, the driver gave us the thumbs up. His tank was full.

The standing Buddha was a beautiful, tall statue, all in gold. There were no other tourists anywhere. We took photos, got a bite to eat, and went to catch our ride back home. But the driver was long gone, so we walked back to our hotel, knowing we'd been taken for a ride. At least it was a free one.

Every human interaction entails some risk. When you travel out of your country, that risk grows, but so does the reward. If you wanted to hedge your bets and never lose, you would never leave home in the first place. That risk is part of the thrill of being abroad: learning new rules, mastering new games.

The trick is to know which ones to avoid at all costs, and which ones you can safely embrace. Chances are you will lose a few and win a few, or at least come out even. You will meet many more good people than bad. But if you do meet someone who outsmarts you, don't let it ruin your day, or your trip.

Because, as my father-in-law said after he'd paid his dues in that Greek bar, "I figured it was just the price of a good story."

January 2012

18

Give and take: On gift-giving

Last year I traveled to Nigeria, where I knew some people, and where I also had some work to do. Before I left, I racked my brain for small gifts that I could give to friends and others I met along the way. At the time, I was a bit low on funds. I wanted to give something meaningful, useful — and affordable. Because a lot of the people I would be seeing were journalists, I thought a great idea might be flash drives — the storage system of the future! I'd been to Nigeria a few years earlier and had not seen them anywhere.

So I stocked up. When I landed in Lagos, I proudly handed over my gift to a friend who took it, turned it over, and said, "Thanks. I could use another one of these." And he pulled a small handful out of his pocket.

Welcome to the global economy, where everything is available everywhere, and simple abundance is no longer unique to the United States. So much has changed so fast, it often seems that giving gifts isn't as simple as it used to be.

But gift-giving has always been complicated. Fraught, even. In his 1925 essay "The Gift," French anthropologist Marcel Mauss argued that in preindustrial societies, the "gift exchange" was part of a complex social cycle made up of three interlocking obligations: to give, to receive, and to reciprocate.

Mauss believed this was the very foundation of society, because with each gift, many other things were exchanged: loyalty, status, spiritual heft, future goodwill. Giving gifts was a complex form of gamesmanship, and the trade in debts of generosity helped strengthen social bonds. In the potlatch tradition among Native Americans of the Pacific Northwest, for instance, leaders competed to give away the greatest number of possessions in exchange for the highest honor. As Mauss saw it, the practice of giving and receiving gifts developed as a way to grease the wheels of the social machine — and there were always strings attached.

That may seem like a cynical view of human nature, but we know now — thanks to the work of scientists including Robert Axelrod, who used computer models to show how cooperation can evolve, and Robert Trivers, who first formalized the idea of "reciprocal altruism" — that the idea of reciprocity is embedded deep in our brains. The cash system has streamlined many exchanges, but giving and receiving still constitute the basic currency of our lives.

Every society has its own rules — often unspoken and hard to decipher — governing how and when gifts are to be exchanged. In Japan, showing up at someone's house without a gift can be considered rude. In Singapore, a gift is often refused three times before being accepted. In Islamic cultures, gifts should be presented — and accepted — with either the right hand only, or both hands. And in many countries, a gift of a sharp object can cut a relationship off.

Negotiating the gift-giving intricacies of a new culture can be unsettling, because you don't know what is expected or what is owed. I got a taste of this when I lived in Tanzania, where people I barely knew asked me for all sorts of things: Can I have this book? Can I have this backpack? I kept a list of everything I was asked for — shoes, bicycles, motorcycles, cars, pens, radios, tuition, sweaters, airfare to America, a girlfriend/fiancée from America, money for seeds, bags of cement, my glasses, the watch off my wrist, the food I was eating, "anything I might have."

This was disturbing at some level. But I also experienced the flip side one day as I was walking down the road from my house, and a man about my age came up the hill eating a handful of peanuts. I said hello. He said hello. Then he held out his hand. *"Karibu karanga,"* he said as we passed each other — literally, "Welcome peanuts." I held out my hand, and he gave me half his nuts. I thanked him and we each moved on, and I never saw him again.

After a few missteps, I got used to the way gifts flowed back and forth more freely than in my own culture. But even though bungling the gift exchange is part of learning how an unfamiliar culture works, it's something you don't have time to do when you're in a new place for a short time. So what gifts are appropriate to bring along as you head out on your travels?

Do a little research on the customs of your destination, but a good rule of thumb is to buy locally to give globally. Don't buy things made in China to give to people who live in China. Don't buy flash drives that are shipped all over the world in vast quantities. Instead, focus on things you can only find where you live: Local foods and drinks, emblems of your town's sports team, a photography book showcasing the beauty of your area. You might even head to the farmers market or county fair. Recently, an old friend visited from Italy, bringing us some cheese and meat, a couple of soccer jerseys, and a leather bag from a famous Italian company. But also consider what people are coveting. Another friend of mine is going to Mecca this year, and he will bring an iPod for his host, because those are hard to get in Saudi Arabia.

Whatever gifts you end up giving likely will be valued and appreciated. Even if you don't get it exactly right, just by giving something, you won't get it completely wrong. Because even Marcel Mauss would acknowledge that the gift itself is not the most important thing. It is a gesture that tells the recipient that the connection between you means something.

In other words, it's the thought that counts.

December 2010

Sleep tight: On bedbugs

Long before bedbugs had become the plague du jour, my wife and I set off for New Zealand. The year was 2000, and we arrived in April to pick apples for a couple of months before buying a barely running car to get us around. We slept in hostels, which had comment books filled with advice about where to stay — and where not to. Many of the entries mentioned bedbugs, which we assumed must be a creature native to New Zealand.

"Whatever you do, don't stay at … (unless you want to be eaten alive by bedbugs — 122 bites to be precise)," warned one entry. By then, we had already stayed there and had each gotten a few bites, but we hadn't thought much about it.

I didn't know it then, but we were close to — in fact, right across the Tasman Sea from — the launching pad for an imminent worldwide explosion of bedbugs.

"Australian hotels had a big bedbug problem going into 2000," says New York City exterminator Jeff Eisenberg, author of *The Bed Bug Survival Guide: The Only Book You Need to Eliminate or Avoid This Pest Now*, when I phoned him at his office recently. "For some reason, they weren't dealing with the issue or didn't take it seriously. Then, after the 2000 Summer Olympics in Sydney, you had thousands of people bringing bedbugs back to their countries, all over the world. The year 2000 was definitely a tipping point."

Two years later, my wife and I moved to Southeast Asia. In our first few days of staying in this budget travel mecca, I noticed some small insects in the rooms. Back then, I thought they were very small cockroaches. Now I don't.

We didn't know anything about the Australian bedbug outbreak, nor had we seen the few articles about the bedbug resurgence that had appeared in medical journals. But one day, I found myself in Sarawak, on the island of Borneo, staying at the only place I could afford, a run-down hostel where the dorm room had a sickly sweet smell that gave me an uneasy feeling. Late that night, I woke up to find the source: The room was absolutely crawling with bedbugs. I put my backpack in its travel sack, tied it tight, and spent a restless night. The next day I fled.

Somehow, every time we encountered the bugs, we managed to not transport them back home. We barely thought about them until around 2005, when the United States — and particularly New York City — shifted into full-fledged bedbug panic mode, as people realized that the little bloodsuckers were staging a massive comeback after 50 years of biding their time, nibbling on other creatures in the shadows or hanging out in the land down under.

By 2010, 95 percent of all U.S. pest control companies had reported bedbug infestations. Eisenberg estimates that by this year, 85 percent of all the buildings in New York City will have had a bedbug problem. He says that infestations tripled in Chicago from 2007 to 2008, and reports are up 70 percent nationwide.

For those of us who travel, this is obviously of some concern. There are few things more unpleasant than finding you've become intimate with a parasite. But as the flood of news stories attests, there are also few things as irresistibly, grotesquely fascinating.

Bedbugs are remarkable critters. They are thought to have evolved from cave-dwelling insects that began feeding on the bats hanging overhead, who then presumably gave them a lift out into the world. They were reported in ancient Egypt, Greece, and Rome, and made appearances in the plays of Aristophanes and Shakespeare. In the 17th century, bedbugs even gave rise to the first professional exterminator: Tiffin & Son, Bug Destroyers to Her Majesty.

They can fit into a crack the size of a business card and survive up to a year (some say 18 months) without blood. They reproduce by way of "traumatic insemination," whereby the male simply pierces the female's side, which seems a little low, even for a bedbug. In many countries, the second half of the 20th century was blissfully bedbug-free. Now it looks to have been a mere lull, an interlude in human history.

It's probably unfair to place all the blame on Australia; even before the outbreak there, the bugs were busy plotting their return. Eisenberg remembers getting his first call about bedbugs in 1996. It was from a hostel in New York City where people were complaining about bites in the night. After a few hours of searching, he found a bedbug, but had to ask an entomologist what it was. Exterminators hadn't seen bedbugs since the 1960s.

Oh, for the innocence of those days. With globalization well underway, bedbugs seem to be here to stay, and Eisenberg says many of us will likely see them in our homes.

While not exactly a fun beach read, *The Bed Bug Survival Guide* is full of useful information on what to do if you do get bedbugs, and how to keep from getting them in the first place. Eisenberg advises putting your mattresses in plastic cases, getting a vacuum cleaner with disposable bags, cleaning weekly, and "cooking" everything that comes into your house either in the clothes dryer or in a PackTite heater. The list is exhaustive — and exhausting — but then again, Eisenberg has never had an infestation at home.

He devotes two chapters to bedbugs and travel, noting: "You should basically assume that you're going to come into contact with bedbugs when you travel." Many hotels, he writes — whether five-star or by-the-hour — do not have an effective plan to control bedbugs.

However, you can check out hotels in advance on websites such as bedbugregistry.com and tripadvisor.com. Among the many precautions Eisenberg advocates are encasing your luggage in something called a BugZip and keeping it in your hotel bathroom (the bugs can't navigate slippery surfaces well).

I started researching this story with a certain amount of trepidation, fearful of what I would learn. About halfway through the book, after reading about all the places you can easily pick up bedbugs (the office, the theater, the bus, the subway, the gym), I started to feel a little empathy for Howard Hughes. I saw bedbugs everywhere and could easily imagine this leading to a need for therapy. Eisenberg warns, however, that even your therapist's couch can harbor bedbugs.

If you lived by every word in Eisenberg's book, you might spend the rest of your life zipped into a plastic bag equipped with a snorkel. But he doesn't advise it. "I don't walk around in a paranoid state all day," he writes. "I live my life. I enjoy myself. I take vacations and sleep in hotels and fly on airplanes."

What he does see a need for is information. "The more people get educated about it," he told me, "the more we'll get a handle on slowing down the spread, knocking out problems in the earlier stages, and not letting things fester as badly as they have."

Some perspective: Humans are perhaps the most successful organism on the planet, and it's only natural that other creatures would hitch their wagon to ours. And while bedbugs may be annoying, embarrassing, and maddening, they don't transmit diseases. They're not even considered a public health threat. Perhaps what they are is a reminder that some things in this world are simply out of our hands.

"You do what you can do," says Eisenberg. "And whatever you can do is better than doing nothing. Just take the basics and go from there."

October 2011

Tipping points: On gratitude and gratuity

"Where is Mr. Frank?"

Mr. Frank was hiding in the back seat of a truck, in the south of Guyana, when he heard the words. He tried to duck down a little, because he knew what was coming.

"Oh," I heard a woman in our group say, "he's over there." She pointed my way. A few moments later, a face appeared in my open window.

"Hello Mr. Frank! Do you have something you can bath me?"

It was Sebastian, the guide who had just hiked up and back down a mountain with our group. We were in a part of the world where tourism had only recently arrived, where not long ago there was barely a cash economy, and where people's English, although it is the country's official language, was not always so good.

"Bath you?" I asked.

"Yes," he said.

I puzzled over the word for a second, but I already knew what he meant. I nodded wearily and dug in my pockets for some money — not a lot, but then again, maybe too much. I had no idea. We'd been told that at the end of the trip, we would give a group tip that would be divided among all the guides who had helped us. But the rules with these things were murky.

"Thank you!" Sebastian said, and he seemed overly happy with the amount. It's not that I didn't want to give it. And I liked Sebastian. I knew he had two daughters and a son. I knew he was just a few years older than me but looked about twice my age. In a way, it felt like I was helping out a friend.

But in another way, it felt like I was paying someone to be my friend. Somehow, it cheapened the small relationship we'd managed to forge. Or maybe it just clarified it. After all, would Sebastian have hiked eight hours, made our shelter, cooked our meals, then walked back down, for free?

Was our relationship real? Was it merely financial? Could it be both? Back home in Minnesota, I ask myself these questions every time I see a tip jar. I tip generously at coffee shops, and to bellmen on the rare occasions that I'm at a hotel. My wife, who once waited tables for $2 an hour, always insists on 20 percent at restaurants, even when the service is less than stellar.

Tipping doesn't bother me. What does bother me is that I don't understand it. I don't know what is being bought or sold, even though I have worked for tips myself. Is a tip a wage? A gift? Charity?

The most common explanation for tipping is that it's a reward for good service. This is what people tell themselves as they hand over their money. This is what servers tell themselves as they take it.

But the research doesn't bear this out. Instead, it shows that the correlation between good service and good tips is very weak. Why, then, does this massive segment of the economy ($44 billion in U.S. restaurants alone) even exist?

There is no consensus on when and where the practice of tipping — or even the word — originated. One common theory is that it first appeared in the 1500s in England, where signs on boxes in coffeehouses purportedly said, "To Insure Promptitude." Other theories trace the word to the Dutch "tippen" (for tapping a coin on a table), or the Roma "tipper me" (meaning "give me"), or the English word for drinking, "tipple."

Wherever it came from, the practice thrived in a stratified England, where visitors to private residences were expected to tip the footmen, valets, and servants. Tipping expanded to hotels and restaurants, and by the 1700s the custom had spread throughout Europe.

Tipping was unknown in America until after the Civil War, when those who wanted to show their worldliness began to import the practice. But the country, apparently, was ripe for it, because by 1900 tipping was well established, with rates in American restaurants, at 10 percent, double those in Europe. Some states tried to ban tipping, arguing that it degraded people and made them grovel for favors rather than work for an honest wage.

There's something to that argument, as I know from my time as a bellman, standing outside a run-down hotel in Portland, Oregon, hauling bags for a dollar — which I always accepted with feigned surprise and gratitude, but to which I felt absolutely entitled. I remember the helpless rage of getting stiffed, as well as the feeling, on good nights, that I had gotten away with something. I loved the tips but was never sure what to make of the tipping.

My experience confirms what the research says: Tipping does not improve service. According to Ofer Azar of Israel's Ben-Gurion University, who has studied this issue, tipping most likely started as a reward, but quickly became a social norm. Azar's research shows that the most common reported reasons for tipping are to show gratitude, to conform to the social norm, and to help supplement a server's income.

This last reason, to me, is the most interesting. There is a theory that we feel anxiety or stress when our relationships with others are unequal, and tipping is a way to restore that balance. Tipping is not simply an economic transaction. It is a complex social and emotional exchange.

Countries that have higher degrees of extroversion (such as the United States), neuroticism (Greece), and status differences (India) tip more often, as do those that emphasize individualism and masculinity (Mexico). Conversely, tipping tends to be more limited in countries that place a higher value on equality (New Zealand), and those that emphasize social relationships over economic ones (Japan).

All of that presents problems for the traveler, who may not understand the social landscape in an unfamiliar country, and whose perception of inequality is likely to be skewed. For example, in Bangladesh, where you will meet lots of poor people, restaurant tipping rates are only about 5 percent. In Japan, meanwhile, people consider tips insulting. In Iran, you will see a service charge, but people will still expect you to tip. In parts of the United States, tip inflation is pushing rates up to 25 percent.

In Guyana, I muddled my way through. I happily gave Hendricks, another of our guides (who laughed at my jokes), some money to buy tin sheets for his roof. I dug deep into my pockets for Wally, the guide who spent the whole week with us, and whom we all loved. After our city-tour guide, David, drove me all over as I tried to buy a phone, he seemed surprised and a little sheepish as I handed him some cash, and I wondered if I had made a misstep.

As we shook hands and he drove away, I hoped what I gave him was enough to pay whatever invisible debt I had incurred and to help bridge the gap between us, but not so much that it would be the only bridge.

September 2011

The food less traveled: On miles and meals

The best meal I ever ate was at a roadside restaurant in the middle of Nigeria. I was in a microbus heading north through an otherworldly landscape strewn with giant boulders. It was mid-morning when we pulled over at an open-air restaurant. The counter where people were ordering was jammed. An old man, seeing my confusion, explained the menu and ordered for me.

We sat down, and the waiter brought our food: a ball of pounded yam and a bowl of egusi soup, made with crushed melon seeds and containing a hunk of beef. The waiter asked if I wanted utensils. I looked around. No one else had them.

The old man leaned over. "You know," he remarked, "they say your food tastes better when you eat it with your hands."

So I waved the waiter off, broke off a piece of yam, dipped it in the soup, and scooped up a piece of the meat. It all melted together in my mouth, sweet, savory, and delicious. The meat was tender and rich from stewing in a sauce.

Sometimes I still wonder why that meal was so transcendent. I was very hungry, but that can't have been the whole reason. It must have had something to do with the experience with the people, the place, the journey itself. Of the 5,000 or so meals I've eaten in my life so far, only a few stand out in my mind. Most of those I've eaten while traveling.

I remember, for example, sitting with my wife in a field next to the Cloudy Bay Vineyards in Marlborough, New Zealand, with some cheese and bread. In the tasting room, we'd emptied our pockets and pushed a pile of change across the counter for the cheapest bottle of sauvignon blanc they had. We lay in the grass, gazing at the mountains in the distance, sipping one of the best wines in the world. I can still taste its fruity crispness. I felt the same sense of perfection at a pizzeria in Italy and at a tiny hole-in-the-wall restaurant in Thailand.

Some meals, of course, are memorable for less idyllic reasons. In Tanzania, where I was teaching school, we were once served rice with a kind of cow stew poured over it. Dora, the other American teacher, leaned over to me.

"Do you want these?" she asked, pointing to some large meaty tubes and a bit of stomach lining.

"Sure," I said. When no one was looking, she forked them onto my plate. I ate them happily.

Strange food can be one of the great joys of travel, but there's an art to eating it. It has to do with letting go of what you think food should be, and being open to what it is. If you can do this, you will be rewarded with an expanded sense of what you can love. You will also, with any luck, develop a strong stomach.

Even then, food may sometimes defeat you. On my way through Burkina Faso in West Africa, my bus pulled over near some vendors, and everyone climbed down to get something to eat. Cuts of goat and sheep sizzled on a grill. I got a packet of mutton wrapped in newspaper, which was salty and delicious. But I was still hungry, so I pointed to something else, which was half the price. This seemed like a bargain until I realized after a few bites that I'd ordered a kind of meat Twinkie: a creamy fat center encased in a golden layer of tripe. It remains one of the few things I haven't been able to finish.

The search for new and different flavors has long been one of the great joys of travel. In fact, the quest for flavors helped drive the age of exploration. When Vasco da Gama landed on the Malabar Coast of India, he was asked what he'd come for. He said, "Christ and spices." Columbus headed west for the same reason, and when Magellan's ship arrived in Spain in 1522 (without Magellan) after sailing around the world, it was loaded down with spices.

Travel is written in the food in front of you. If you go to Bologna, Italy, you might order lasagna in hopes of eating an authentic Italian meal. And it is one, except that two of the main ingredients are not native to Italy. Pasta arrived from North Africa in the early Middle Ages, and the tomato, which came from the Americas along with potatoes, corn, peppers, avocados, and squash, didn't appear in Italian recipes until the 1700s, and was originally called *pomo di moro*, or "apple of the Moors."

Everywhere people have traveled, conquered, or proselytized, they have left culinary tracks. The baguette is sold all across French-speaking West Africa, where it's sliced open and slathered with meats and sauces. In former French colonies like Vietnam and Cambodia, you will find those same baguettes filled with pate, cilantro, marinated meat, and vegetables. Across East Africa, corn is a staple of local diets, often ground and made into a kind of porridge. In Somalia, the Italian and Indian influences have led to dishes such as pasta with goat meat and mild curries.

As I walk around Minneapolis, where I live now, I inhale the smells of kitchens from around the world. I stroll through Asian grocery stores and wonder at the fish balls and giant waterbugs. At a little Vietnamese restaurant where no English is spoken, I stop in regularly for the banh mi sandwich. At an East African restaurant not far from my house, the ugali (stiff maize porridge) and nyama choma (roasted meat) bring me closer to Tanzania than I've been in many years.

And that is what I love most about food — when opening my mouth means opening my mind, and I'm transported into another world.

November 2011

Walk this way: On getting around

My wife, Bridgit, and I were cruising down the west coast of New Zealand in a barely running car. It was the second half of our grand kiwi tour. We'd bought the car for next to nothing from another picker in the orchard where we'd just finished working. When the apple season started winding down, we began tooling around the islands, burning through the money we'd earned.

It was idyllic. It was also a lot of togetherness. As the days wore on, our conversations in that car became punctuated with increasingly blunt comments (mostly from Bridgit), like "I want you to know that I'm not enjoying this" and "Let's not turn funny into annoying, OK?"

But public transportation was minimal, and tourist buses were expensive. And the islands of New Zealand are, we learned, pretty big. So the cramped old car was our only option.

Getting yourself from one place to another is one of the most stressful parts of traveling. You board the wrong bus. You pay far too much for a taxi. You miss your train. You end up in towns you've never heard of (and quickly realize why that is).

You can treat this as an annoyance or as an opportunity. Learning how people move themselves around can tell you as much about their city or country as its food or its art or its history can. It can change the way you see that place.

A few years after our New Zealand adventure, we lived in Bangkok, Thailand. Below our apartment window ran one of the city's few remaining canals. I would sit and watch the big boats speed up and down, barely stopping to let commuters jump off at the docks. The water was gray and garbage-filled. Yet children swam in those canals, and once we saw a 3-foot lizard crawl out of the water and into the trees. Somehow the canals still held life, and history. Gazing out my window, I would try to imagine the time when the waterways snaked across the entire city — when Bangkok was known more for its canals than for anything else.

These days, unless we blow a tire or miss a flight, we don't really think about transportation. But for a long time, it was one of humanity's greatest challenges. People moved from place to place so slowly and deliberately that there was even a saying: "The soul moves at the speed of a camel."

Our modern ability to move abruptly from one continent to another must be one of the primary causes of culture shock. In the space of a few hours, we can find ourselves immersed in a world that, over thousands of years, has evolved differently from the one we left. In Tanzania, I lived in a house at the top of long dirt road. I didn't have a car, so whenever I wanted to go anywhere, I had to walk. At first, this seemed hellish. After a lifetime of getting around by car in the United States, walking seemed like an incredible waste of time and energy. Picking up groceries took half a day, sometimes longer. Running any errand, in fact, required a major expedition.

And yet, as a walker, I was a part of local life. After a few months, the hourlong trek to town didn't seem so far. Besides, that road was how I met my neighbors, and how I got invited into their homes. It was how I found out who their children were. If I hadn't been forced to walk, I'm afraid I would have stayed hidden away in my house.

The idea that the way you move through a place is key to how you experience it has been around since at least the mid-20th century, when French postmodern intellectual circles influenced, and were influenced by, movements such as dadaism, surrealism, lettrism, and situationism. Guy Debord, a theorist from this last camp, came up with the word *psychogeography* to describe the interaction of place and mind. According to the British novelist Will Self, author of the 2007 book *Psychogeography*, the idea was rooted in the French concept of the flâneur (sometimes translated as "stroller" or "drifter").

Psychogeography has undergone something of a mini renaissance with Self's book, which details epic walks he's undertaken, including a stroll from John F. Kennedy Airport in Queens to Manhattan. Another, more scholarly, work of the same title by Merlin Coverly came out in 2006, and the *Lonely Planet Guide to Experimental Travel* landed in bookstores a few years ago. German filmmaker Werner Herzog has said, "Tourism is sin, and travel on foot virtue." I wouldn't go so far as that, but I do believe that the way you physically maneuver through a city or country profoundly affects your knowledge and understanding of it.

Figuring out how to get around, maddening as it may be, is mostly a matter of figuring out the rules. And there are always rules. Not long ago, Bridgit and I were driving through France, reliving the lowest points of our New Zealand trip, when we came to the realization that the names of roads didn't actually matter. What mattered was the name of the towns they led to.

This learning curve can be as steep and treacherous as a mountain road — and as full of icy glares from one's spouse — but the satisfaction that comes with mastering the train or the canal or the bus, or even the car, can make the journey that much more rewarding.

One day during that tour of New Zealand, Bridgit and I pulled into a campsite overlooking the Tasman Sea. We were tired. It was late. There had been sniping.

We set up our tent and trudged up to the communal kitchen to cook dinner.

When we came back, Bridgit tried to open the trunk.

"Do you have the key?" she asked.

"Um," I said.

"Don't tell me."

I didn't need to. Other than our tent and some dirty dishes, everything we had was in the locked car, including our only key.

The campground owner showed us how to jimmy the front door open. Once we were in, we pulled out the back seat and found a hole just big enough for one arm. I spent the rest of the night emptying the trunk — item by item — until we finally pulled out our sleeping bags and called it a day.

The next morning, the wind off the ocean was cool and fresh. I started digging in the trunk again and soon heard a promising jingle. Before long, we were back on the road, which seemed bright and fast and full of promise.

July 2012

Cultural immersion: On travel and deep reading

About 10 years ago, as I was planning a trip to Kenya and looking for something to read on the plane, I picked up a copy of a book called *A Game of Thrones*. This was before the television show, and I didn't know much about the book, but it struck me as the perfect kind of escape for the journey across the Atlantic, or after a long day navigating Nairobi's streets.

As the plane lifted off, I was immediately pulled into the world of the book so deeply that when I looked up, I was surprised to find myself 30,000 feet in the air. It was complete immersion — a journey within a journey. I finished the book a few days after landing, then spent way too much time searching bookshops throughout the city for the sequel, which I eventually found at a mall in the Nairobi suburbs. Upon my return to the United States, I bought the third book in the series on my way out of the airport.

To date, that reading experience remains one of the most satisfying of my life. I look back on my journey through Westeros almost as fondly as my journey through East Africa.

And it was not the first time I'd had an experience like that. There is something about the sealed chamber of an airplane — and about travel in general — that lends itself to immersive reading.

Some years earlier, when I first arrived in East Africa to teach English in Tanzania, I brought a few books along. One of these was *Dune*, by Frank Herbert, which I devoured in about three days while at the language school where we teachers were studying Swahili. Another was Michael Crichton's *Jurassic Park*, which I took on a trip to Nairobi; I can still remember becoming lost in it while sitting in my crappy hotel room.

I can still recall scenes from those books — and what it felt like to be so deeply immersed in them. But it wasn't just escapist fiction that had this effect. When my wife and I were living in Thailand, where we'd moved to teach English, I spent days in our Bangkok apartment poring over Steven Pinker's *The Blank Slate*, on the theory of human nature, like it was some sort of thriller. When I was stuck in a hospital in Tanzania after having my appendix out, I devoured Joseph Campbell's collection of essays *Myths to Live By*, and then proceeded to live by those myths. And when I first arrived at college — just back from a year as an exchange student in Italy and experiencing my own culture like a foreign one — I read Henry David Thoreau's *Walden* for a class assignment. Its effect on me was profound: Ever since, I have tried to value time over money and experience over things, and to be mindful that (to paraphrase), when I come to die, I do not discover that I have not lived.

One reason books and travel mix so well might be that in another country, in another culture, in another language, all your familiar cues are gone. All your assumptions are challenged. Your expectations for how things should go are useless. The mindless scripts that you follow every day in your interactions are torn up and blown away. The ground under your feet is constantly shifting.

This creates the perfect conditions for what Diana Pasulka, a professor of religion at the University of North Carolina, Wilmington, calls the "book encounter," which she describes as that moment in time when your internal state is perfectly aligned to be receptive to a particular book. When that happens, and you reach the end, the world feels different.

Pasulka agrees that there's something about being abroad that can facilitate the book encounter. Her most profound experience with it happened closer to home, though, in graduate school. Friends had been telling her she needed to read the philosopher Friedrich Nietzsche, and although she had tried a few times, his writings didn't click. She didn't get it. She didn't like him.

Then, late one New Year's Eve, Pasulka was awakened by the sound of partying outside her room. On her nightstand was Nietzsche's *The Gay Science*. Unable to get back to sleep, she picked up the book and by chance opened it to a section called "Sanctus Januarius," which was about New Year's Eve and making declarations for the new year.

Well, she thought, that's strange. What a coincidence!

Then she turned the page to find a passage admonishing her not to trust coincidences. Pasulka was stunned.

"I honestly felt like the book was alive at that point," Pasulka said when I called her to ask about this. "I just looked at it like, 'Wow. This is powerful.'"

Pasulka wrote her doctoral dissertation on the practice of "deep reading" in religious traditions, known in Christianity as *lectio divina*. This refers to the act of devoting the full force of your attention to a text in order to absorb the truths it holds. When she researched belief in UFOs as a kind of religious faith for her 2019 book *American Cosmic: UFOs, Religion, Technology*, she found that reading books this way often plays a role in semireligious conversions, such as accepting the belief that UFOs are alien spacecraft.

"The book encounter is a full experience of life," Pasulka says. "It's not just getting information from this book; it's that this book becomes part of you. It's creating a kind of interpretive framework for your life — why you're here and what you're doing."

Looking back over my own book encounters, it's hard not to notice how many of them took place when I was younger. Maybe that's because I had more time for introspection — no kids to shuttle, no leaking dishwashers to fix. Or maybe it's because when we're younger, we read for a different reason. We are trying to figure out how the world works and our place in it. We are trying to understand the stories unfolding around us, but also what our own story is and how it intersects with all those other stories.

As the years pass, however, those questions do not burn quite as hot, and the possibilities for how your life will turn out grow narrower. Maybe the window for the book encounter becomes smaller as we age. That would help explain the more mundane list of books that have affected me in recent years, like *Getting Things Done, Deep Work,* and *Positivity.*

Or maybe it's just the arithmetic of attention: The more things you are attending to at any given point, the less impact any of them can have. But when you're traveling, your life is pared down to a few simple goals: getting to where you're going, finding something to eat and a place to sleep. There are fewer things to be done, so the amount of attention you can devote to a book is greater.

Outside of travel, that kind of focus can be hard to find. And as connected technology creeps into every corner of our lives, even the airplane seat now offers a few hundred movies and Wi-Fi. For those who love the way books can change us, such distractions are alarming.

"We are short-circuiting the deep-reading brain," says Maryanne Wolf, author of *Reader, Come Home: The Reading Brain in a Digital World.* Wolf is the director of the Center for Dyslexia, Diverse Learners, and Social Justice at UCLA, and she is worried about the loss of our ability — including her own — to read deeply. As she points out, reading is something we must practice.

"When the brain learns to read, it's doing something unnatural," Wolf says. "Our species was absolutely made to speak, to think, to see, to smell. But it has not a single gene that is specific to reading. So what it has to do is build a new circuit."

Recently, Wolf realized that she was losing her capacity for deep reading. So she took the step of implementing a practice similar to *lectio divina* to try to maintain those skills. Every morning, she takes a few pages on a subject that she doesn't know well and reads them, deeply. Before she goes to bed, she does the same.

"The deep-reading processes take more time," Wolf says. "We're talking milliseconds, not minutes, but we don't give enough milliseconds to all those critical, analytic processes. When you skim, you skip — but you don't just skip words. You skip the deep-reading processes."

Deep reading is something I never want to skip, whether I'm in an airplane high above the ocean or at home sitting on my couch. Because there is a kind of magic in books — and in that moment when your inner and outer worlds align in some new way, your world can be transformed.

Yet no matter how far we travel, or what culture we find ourselves in, books can only meet us halfway. Whether we make the rest of the journey is up to us.

July 2021

Photographic Memory: On the Purpose of Pixels

In the middle of Hong Kong Island is a mountain known as the Peak. A cable car climbs the slope from the city, arriving at a building called the Peak Tower. Take the escalators to the top and you'll find one of the most breathtaking views in the world.

On one side is the forest of skyscrapers that makes up the megacity of Hong Kong. On the other, trees cover the mountain as it sweeps down to the ocean, which itself stretches out to the horizon. A cool wind from the sea washes over Peak Tower, and on the currents above, raptors drift, looking for prey. Below, through Hong Kong's hazy air, helicopters fly, and further out boats slip through the harbor across giant waves that look almost gentle from the Peak.

I stood there for almost two hours when I was in Hong Kong recently. I didn't want the experience to end. I wanted to soak it up, not knowing if I would be back. I took a few photos, but most of the time I just looked out over the edge.

Before long, the other tourists in my group left and new ones arrived. This happened several times, and the more I watched, the more puzzled I became. Over and over, I saw people stand at the edge with their phones and cameras. They would take one picture, look at it, delete it, then take another.

Some people did this again and again until they got the right one. When satisfied, they left. Another time, I watched an entire family take some photos, then sit down on a bench and stare at their phones for half an hour. They barely seemed to know where they were.

Were they really present on the Peak Tower? Or were they only partly there and partly elsewhere, lost in "the cloud" where they could post their pictures for everyone to see? Was this simply a performance for their online audience? Were they so desperate to capture an experience that they were willing to not even have it?

I worked myself up into a state over this, and since then, I have given this phenomenon a lot of thought. It seems we are afraid that if we can't capture an image of an experience, it wasn't real. The quantity of photographs we take every day is staggering: 60 million posted to Instagram, 350 million uploaded to Facebook, 400 million added to Snapchat. One 2012 estimate put the number of -photos taken on mobile phones at 1.4 billion every day.

"The possession of a camera can inspire something akin to lust," Susan Sontag wrote in her 1977 treatise On Photography. "And like all credible forms of lust, it cannot be satisfied: first because the possibilities of photography are infinite; and second, because the project is finally self-devouring."

This becomes an issue when we are out in the world. "Travel becomes a strategy for accumulating photographs," Sontag wrote. "A way of certifying experience, taking photographs is also a way of refusing it."

While photos used to be seen as a way of documenting a journey, they now risk becoming the point of it. It's a departure from older notions of travel, in which the ostensible purpose was to take in new things, to let them become part of you, and to make you a richer, more interesting, possibly even wiser person. That line of thinking can be traced back through Jack Kerouac to Mark Twain to Henry David Thoreau, who wanted to live deliberately, not to have pictures of himself doing it.

Linda Henkel, a memory researcher at Fairfield University in Connecticut, has been researching the effect of photo-taking on memory. "I was interested in exactly this issue," she told me when I called her. "We have a beautiful museum on campus, and people go there and take photographs of things. But when you watch them doing it, they barely look at the objects."

In a study she designed, Henkel took 27 undergraduates and had them go to the museum, where they photographed 15 items and observed 15 others. The next day, they were tested on which objects they remembered seeing. "What we found," she says, "was that people remembered fewer of the objects — and they remembered fewer details about an object — if they had taken a photograph of it than if they had just looked at it. So the act of taking a photograph actually impaired their memory."

What's most likely at work here (in addition to divided attention), she says, is what's called "directed -forgetting," where we tell our brain that it doesn't need to remember something. "Once we hit that button," she says, "it's as if we're sending a signal to our brain: You don't have to think about this, you don't have to process this, you don't have to consolidate it, because the camera is going to store the information."

Photographs, of course, are good at capturing details we might not otherwise remember, and for documenting things we need to report on. Some technology enthusiasts say this is precisely the point: We can store information electronically, freeing up our minds for other uses. They call this "distributed cognition," and maintain that expanded digital memory effectively increases our intelligence.

But with smartphones and digital photography, we take far more photos than we could ever organize or look at. "People have a thousand photos on their smartphones," Henkel says, "and they're overwhelmed with trying to go through them and look at them. So they collect the photographs but don't actually use them. And collecting photographs isn't going to benefit memory."

More to the point, a photo and a memory are different things. To create a memory from an experience, you need to engage in the process of turning it into something richer and more meaningful than a bunch of pixels. You need to come back to it, think about it, and remember it. Henkel recommends that we take fewer -photos and be more deliberate about the ones we do take. Then we should find other ways of layering meaning onto our memories — by writing about them, reflecting on them, and sharing them with people in our lives, and not only online.

"Photographs are wonderful memory tools," she says. "I still take photos. But if you want to better remember an experience, focus on the experience itself and then supplement it, so the photographs serve as cues to the key aspects. That's what will lead to the richest memory traces."

The photos we take should be like signs that point down the path to our memories. The things outside the frame are what give an experience the texture that makes it real. The memory I have of the Peak Tower, for example, contains so many things, including the sun and the wind and a feeling of wonder, all of which I will never forget. And for me, that's worth far more than a thousand words, or even a million likes.

October 2014

The rewards of risk: On freedom and fear

A few years ago in his Los Angeles home, a man named Dave Freeman fell, hit his head, and died. This wouldn't have been big news, except that the 47-year-old Freeman had launched what became an entire genre of books when, in 1999, he and a friend published *100 Things to Do Before You Die*. In it, they exhorted people to get out and experience things like the Namaqualand wildflower bloom in South Africa, or a voodoo pilgrimage in Haiti, or the Fringe Festival Nude Night Surfing competition in Australia.

Before his death, if I thought about Freeman at all, it was to dismiss his book as a gimmicky Christmas present you might get from an aunt who doesn't know you very well. But since his demise, I have found my thoughts returning to him and his project.

"This life is a short journey," Freeman wrote in the introduction, then told the reader to "get off your butt and create a fabulous memory or two" before it was over. It was a call to arms against complacency, a prod to approach life as a beast to be wrestled to the ground rather than one to be led placidly to the stockade.

This way of living didn't, however, come without risk. "Be warned," Freeman noted, "that aside from having fun, you could be crushed, gored, burned, frozen, drowned, run over, electrocuted, infected, punctured, or dehydrated. You could get hit with a mallet, arrow, or pumpkin. ... So be careful. And don't say we didn't warn you."

The tongue-in-cheek disclaimer was probably enough to send many armchair travelers back to their La-Z-Boys. Yet it also made a serious point: Travel can be risky. The world can be dangerous, and you never know what you will encounter. What Freeman didn't say, though — and perhaps didn't even realize — was that many of the things he was writing about are exhilarating not in spite of the risk, but because of it.

Frank Farley, a professor of psychology at Temple University, is an expert on the psychology of risk and says that the more he researches it, the more he sees it as the essential ingredient of life. "Helen Keller would say over and over, 'Life is either a daring adventure, or nothing,'" Farley told me. "How many people don't view life that way? They view life as a series of dangers to be avoided. Nuclear war. Toxic environment. Bad food. Danger in the streets. They focus more on the things to be avoided than on the things for which we should live."

This, he thinks, is a recipe for disappointment. "So many people in their last days realize, 'My God, it's over and I never really lived.' And that's got to be an awful mental state to be in."

Farley has divided personalities into two types. There are what he calls "big-T" people, who seek challenges and who "let go of life's handrails," as he puts it. They enjoy the thrill ("T") of seeing what they can do. Some are "T-Mental" (Albert Einstein) and others are "T-Physical" (Evel Knievel). Some people veer into more destructive risks, such as gambling and crime; he refers to them as "T-Negative."

Then there are what Farley calls "small-t" types — people who are risk-averse, who let their lives be circumscribed by what they fear: failure, loss, humiliation, pain. They avoid these things at all costs. "We can get tied up with fears — a little fear here, a little fear here, and a little fear over there — and it adds up," he says. "It begins constricting your life. Ralph Waldo Emerson said, 'Always confront the things you are afraid of.' Risk-taking is the essence of overcoming fear."

Over the last few decades in the United States, as our fears have become disconnected from the reality of our lives, the balance has shifted toward risk aversion. Taylor Clark points out in his 2011 book, *Nerve: Poise Under Pressure, Serenity Under Stress, and the Brave New Science of Fear and Cool*, that Americans are five times more likely to suffer from anxiety (the fear of possible future misfortune) than are Nigerians. In fact, it is now our No. 1 mental health issue, affecting 18 percent of the population.

In his book *The Culture of Fear: Why Americans Are Afraid of the Wrong Things*, sociologist Barry Glassner examines why we are afraid of factors such as crime and plane crashes when the risks they pose to us are statistically small. In the 1990s, two-thirds of Americans thought crime was soaring, when in fact the murder rate dropped 20 percent between 1990 and 1998. (The percentage of TV news stories about those murders, however, grew 600 percent, even excluding stories about O.J. Simpson.)

In another book, also called *Culture of Fear*, British sociologist Frank Füredi says that our fears about society have little to do with actual, empirical risks. "Rather," he writes, "they are shaped by cultural assumptions about human vulnerability." One problem, Füredi notes, is that safety has become an end in itself rather than a means to get on with other things. Another is that our emotional response to danger is seen as legitimate even when the danger isn't real.

What has changed is our view of the universe, and of our place in it. "We find it very hard to deal with uncertainty," Füredi writes, "partly due to the great progress made by medicine and science. Because we have so much knowledge, a chance occurrence is hard to accept — especially if it causes injury."

That makes sense, but it still doesn't explain why, at a time when we are safer and healthier than we've ever been, we feel less so. We live in the world that our great-grandparents dreamed of, yet we seem incapable of enjoying it, unable to let go of those handrails, ever more afraid of the unknown.

When Dave Freeman died, much of the coverage focused on how he had done only about half the things on his list. And while I don't want to turn him into some kind of Jean-Paul Sartre with a plane ticket, I think those people missed the point. What his death should have brought home was the danger not of completing a list halfway, but of not having such a list at all. It should have reminded us that life is a short journey, and you never know when it will end. Not taking risks along the way is the biggest risk of all.

January 2013

CULTURE

One for the road: On travel and creativity (Part I)

After high school, I went to Italy as an exchange student. One day, I was sitting at my host family's dinner table, happily shoving pasta into my mouth and gulping down whole glasses of water, when the eldest daughter, Anna, spoke up.

"You know," she said, "you'll never get a girlfriend if you keep eating like that."

"Eating like what?" I asked.

"Eating like this," she said, and did her best impression of a prehistoric man feeding off a mammoth leg. I got a little defensive.

"What does it matter," I snapped, "as long as the food gets into your mouth?"

"That is so American," she said. "Here it is not like that. For example, Constanza is thinking about breaking up with her boyfriend because his manners are so bad."

"Really?" I asked.

If she wanted to get my attention, she had it: Constanza was her beautiful, dark-haired friend. I had no idea that this was how I was eating, or that it mattered. I didn't have a clue how I looked to others in this place where I was living.

When I tell this story, people tend to think that Anna was a little hard on me. I certainly didn't take her feedback well at the time. But I look back on this lesson with gratitude, because I know that she helped start me on a path toward being a more creative person.

Last year, in one of the first major studies on the effects of living in another country, researchers found that exposure to a different culture may help explain why artists such as Hemingway, Nabokov, and Picasso did their best work either while living abroad or after returning home. Experiencing another culture can, they found, make you more creative.

William Maddux of INSEAD, an international business school and research institution, and Adam D. Galinsky of Northwestern University ran five studies to gauge how well people solve "insight creativity tasks." In the Duncker candle problem, for example, they gave subjects a picture showing a candle, a box of tacks, and a matchbook, and asked them to figure out how to attach the candle to a wall so that, when lit, no wax would drip on the floor. Of those who had lived abroad, 60 percent came up with the creative solution (using the empty box, tacked to the wall, as a candleholder), as compared with 42 percent of those who hadn't lived abroad. Another test required pairs of subjects to creatively negotiate the sale of a gas station when there was a gap between what the "buyer" was willing to pay and what the "seller" was willing to accept. When both subjects had lived in another country, they arrived at an agreement 70 percent of the time. When neither had, they never reached a deal. In yet another test, participants had to draw an alien from another galaxy. Those who had lived abroad drew "more atypical sensory features … less similar to Earth creatures, and were overall more creative."

Maddux and Galinsky not only found a link between living abroad and the ability to solve these problems but also discovered that the more time people had spent in another culture and the better they had adapted to it, the more creative they were. Simply recalling their life abroad gave participants a boost in how creatively they solved the task.

In another recent study, subjects completed a creative writing exercise after watching a slideshow that focused on either American or Chinese culture, or that compared the two. Those who saw the slideshow comparing the cultures wrote more creatively than those who viewed a presentation about only one culture.

Maddux and Galinsky didn't observe the creativity effect that they'd seen in people who had lived in another country among those who had briefly traveled abroad. However, some studies have found that, in general, students are better (and more creative) at problem-solving when they are told that the problems were written by people in another part of the country or the world. Research has shown that having a "multicultural experience" can enhance one's creativity, and that learning a foreign language can benefit the brain in areas ranging from complex thinking to mental flexibility to interpersonal skills.

These effects likely have to do with acquiring what is called reflected knowledge — understanding how you look from another culture's point of view — as well as how much you internalize that view. Reflected knowledge allows you to see things as an outsider. Once people live abroad and learn to see themselves and their culture from afar, those things never look the same again.

This shift in perspective can be a painful process. For me, it started a few days after the incident at the dinner table. By then, I had started to regret my belligerence. In my mind, I kept replaying the image of myself as the caveman dinner guest. I swallowed my pride, went back to Anna, and asked her to teach me proper Italian table manners.

I learned the rules: Take small bites. Sip, don't chug. Don't belch. Don't undo your belt and announce how full you are. And when you're finished, place your knife and fork parallel across your plate.

Taking my first tentative steps outside my own culture, I began to see my language and beliefs and customs as not inherently right or wrong. Once I started down this road, there was no turning back. It became easier to understand other views, other mannerisms, other ways of being. I tried many of these on, in the way an actor tries on different characters. Along the way, my manners improved. And I did get a girlfriend.

But in the end I got much more: I found myself in a world that felt rich and full of possibilities that, if I could find a way to imagine them, were mine to create.

October 2010

Sense and sensitivity: On translation and meaning

It was getting dark. Paulo had been walking with me for half an hour. He'd invited me to dinner at his house, up near Mount Meru, and now we were going back down the dusty road to my neighborhood in Arusha, Tanzania. I wondered when he would turn around. I kept telling him I knew the way. But he kept walking.

"It's okay," he said. "I can escort you."

The last thing I needed was an escort. I enjoyed walking by myself. But I didn't realize how much had been lost in translation between Paulo's chosen English word, "escort," and the Swahili word for what he meant, *kusindikiza*.

In my dictionary, *kusindikiza* signified "to see someone off" or "to accompany someone part of the way home." I had read these definitions, but I didn't really understand them. Why would you want to accompany someone part of the way home? That is often the problem with learning new languages: You are taking an idea from one world and transporting it to another. The edges of the word, the shape of the idea, do not fit neatly into a new box.

Delving into a language is always partly about exploring new emotional terrain and figuring out how new notions go with a new set of words. According to linguist Steven Pinker, this is the essence of language: "People do not think in English or Chinese or Apache," he writes in his book *The Language Instinct*. "They think in a language of thought." Pinker says this is sometimes called "mentalese," and it isn't the same as what we speak. Instead, we translate our thoughts into words, which is why many foreign words are so hard to translate — you need to understand the ideas behind them.

Words in other languages are like icebergs: The basic meaning is visible above the surface, but we can only guess at the shape of the vast chambers of meaning below. And every language has particularly hard-to-translate terms, such as the Portuguese *saudade*, meaning "the feeling of missing someone or something that is gone," or the Japanese *ichigo-ichie*, meaning "the practice of treasuring each moment and trying to make it perfect." Linguists refer to the distance between these words and their rough translations as a lacuna, which comes from the Latin word for "pool" or "lake." There's a space we need to swim across to reach the other side.

For me, this is one of the great joys of traveling the world and learning different ways of thinking, of feeling, and of being: to land on some new shore of the mind, to look around and admire the view.

Of course, not everyone feels this way. A few years ago, a French businessman and thinker named Jean-Paul Nerriere noticed a trend among non-native English speakers he encountered at meetings: They were using a stripped-down version of the language, and they could communicate more easily with each other than with native English speakers. It was as if they had found a way to drain all the lacunas and meet on a tiny island where only the most utilitarian words would be needed.

Nerriere identified about 1,500 of the most essential English words, dubbed this shorthand Globish, and pronounced it a new global language. Now British journalist Robert McCrum, who has written a book called *Globish: How the English Language Became the World's Language*, is claiming that it has passed beyond the sphere of American and British influence and become a "supranational phenomenon." McCrum asserts that Globish will be "the linguistic phenomenon of the 21st century."

He is probably right. Globish will be useful in many ways. But its limits will come to light as people become aware of everything that's not being communicated — that simply cannot be communicated — with a handful of words floating on a vast ocean of feeling. Globish will either grow and morph into something rich and complex, or shrink and die as we realize how many of our thoughts are getting lost in translation, and how many lacunas still separate us.

It takes time and patience to learn the meaning of words in another language. It was only with time that I began to understand the meaning of *kusindikiza*. I learned it when people stopped to talk with me on the road. I learned it when they invited me to sit with them for tea. I learned it when I translated the Swahili proverb *Wageni ni baraka*. It means "guests are a blessing," and I finally understood that people meant it when they said it, and that theirs was a world filled with gestures that showed how they enjoyed your company, how they valued your presence, and how they would walk for miles to show you that your friendship meant something to them.

Those are the feelings that cannot be included in the Swahili-English dictionary and that will baffle Globish speakers, but that are also among the rich rewards waiting on the other side of the lacuna.

Night had fallen on the road from Mount Meru when Paulo finally said goodbye, turned around, and headed back up the hill. I remember feeling bad for making him walk so far. But I also remember feeling strangely good that he had accompanied me all that way. And even now, years later, living in the United States, when I leave a friend's house and hear the door shut behind me, part of me wishes there were someone to walk me halfway home.

August 2010

Time travel: On the shape of time

One recent morning in Nairobi, Kenya, I was sitting in the ninth-floor lobby of a downtown office building, waiting for the Tanzanian High Commission to issue me a visa. Several Kenyans were also waiting. But the office was as empty as a ghost town.

One man, holding a handful of passports for his clients, chuckled. "They are just taking their tea," he said. "Tanzanians love their tea!" Another man looked at his watch and shook his head in disgust. Finally, a woman sauntered down the hallway and sat at a desk. After a few minutes, she looked up, took our passports, and told us to come back at 3:30.

In the elevator on the way down, the Kenyans were fuming. "It's unbelievable," one of them said. "Those people are so lazy."

It might have been unbelievable to them, but it wasn't to me. I had once lived in Tanzania, and one of the most difficult and disorienting things about it was adjusting to Tanzanian notions of time. There, time seemed to expand around events rather than contract to constrain them. Transitions were gentler. The flow was more measured. Things happened in a way that suggested time was not finite, but something of which there was plenty, if you knew the proper way to wait.

Kenya used to be more like that. But Kenya, or at least Nairobi, has changed. What has happened there is the same thing that has happened in the West: The idea of time has grown more linear, more compressed, and more accelerated as it pushes forward into the future.

It's no accident that this has occurred during a period of rapid economic growth. Linear time has been both a product of and a key to industrialization. For several thousand years, sundials, water clocks, and hourglasses measured time well enough, but they had their limits. It wasn't until mechanical timepieces became more accurate that time could be divided and used more efficiently. In the industrialized world, these clocks gave us more control over our day and sent us hurtling into a linear future. In 1934, the U.S. historian and writer Lewis Mumford called the clock "the key machine of the modern industrial age."

Clocks essentially transformed our sense of time into something independent of us, as opposed to something we participated in. Clock time ticked away at the same steady rate regardless of what we did. It was something we could quantify. It allowed us to sever the day precisely into work and play, into personal and professional, into company time and time off. It allowed people to sell minutes of their life the same way they sold widgets. Time became scarce. Time became money. The time we sold was work; the time we didn't sell was ours.

For the last 300 years, this has been the dominant mode of industrial societies. It has been the subject of laws and strikes and riots. But it is not something that comes naturally to us. Before reliable timepieces existed, time was seen as cyclical, as something that would come around again. It was seen as emerging from events themselves, not from a clock on the wall.

These different notions of time can be complex to think about, but they are real. Adapting to a new idea of time was one of the most profound changes I'd undergone while living abroad. And although I'd thought a lot about this phenomenon, I never had the right words for it — until I came across some articles in the journal *Time and Society* that referred to our collection of assumptions about time as our "timescape," a term coined in the 1990s by social scientist Barbara Adam.

A timescape is the shape that time takes in our mind — the way we see it rolling out in front of us and behind us. It is the texture of time as it unfolds. It can feel different in different contexts (work, home, vacation, meetings) or in different cultures. For example, while we may view time as stretching out in front of us and the past trailing behind us, the Aymara people of the Andes refer to the past as being in front of them and the future behind them; that's because the past is something they can see, while the future remains hidden. To celebrate the new year, Madagascar's Malagasy speakers, who also see time this way, say, "Congratulations for being reached by the year."

The issue of "temporal diversity" was at the top of the agenda of the Tutzing Time Ecology Conference in 2000. The researchers — who are part of a German initiative that looks at how time affects society — believed that many of the older, slower timescapes were endangered by the increasing push for time compression and acceleration.

That acceleration was what I saw in the office in Nairobi. And while it may be the cost of wealth, of progress, and of a certain kind of productivity, I can't help agreeing with the Tutzing folks, who concluded that "only by immersing ourselves in each form of time … can we benefit from the variety of forms of time that exist."

The relatively young industrial work-play timescape has undergone a major shift with the rise of connective technology. It has given way to what researchers call the "nonstop society," or "timeless time," in which people are always available and things are more accelerated and compressed than ever. The computer — the invention that allowed us so much more control over our lives — seems also to have taken it away.

But this trend has not yet made it to the ninth-floor office of the Tanzanian High Commission. When I showed up at 3:30, there was, of course, no one there. In the lobby, three window washers sat with their ropes, waiting to get paid. It was hard to tell whether they thought they were wasting time or felt they had plenty.

I did have other things I wanted to do. But as the minutes ticked by and I found myself looking at my own watch, I tried to remind myself what I had learned all those years ago. Time is money, yes. But time can be many other things. I tried to bend my mind backward, and I could almost get into that other place, where things weren't quite so urgent. It felt different, better, gentler. It was a place where time felt like life.

September 2012

The ecology of money: On power and a pastor

"America," said the exercise in our grammar book, "is the (rich) country in the world." It was a lesson about the superlative, and the answer was, of course, "richest." I was teaching English in Tanzania, and it was strange to read such things about my home.

"You are a rich man," one of my students was fond of telling me, exasperated because I wouldn't give him the books, pens, pencils, and notebooks he asked for. "But you are a rich man. America is a rich country." He seemed to take a certain relish in using the word as he rolled the r, drew out the i, and let the ch trail off. "Reech…"

This bothered me. It felt like an accusation. It made me resent something that was larger than myself, something that I had nothing to do with — something that wasn't my fault.

Why did I get so angry? I spent a lot of time agonizing over that question. It seemed to come from the guilt that many of us feel when we cross a border into a poorer country. After a lifetime of being average, we find ourselves bizarrely privileged. Suddenly we become one of the global elite.

This affects our relationships with the people we meet. Even as a barely out of college kid with some money I'd saved working part-time jobs, within days of moving into my house in Tanzania (provided by the teaching program), I had a steady stream of people coming to my door asking if I needed a gardener, or a night guard, or a cook, or someone to clean the house. Everyone wanted a job or had a brother, sister, or friend who did. I had the money, so I was boss.

Reactions varied among my fellow foreigners. Some shrugged it off. Some struggled to rationalize it. Some felt a constant, nagging guilt about it. A few reveled in it. For my part, I mostly tried to understand it. Exactly what, I asked myself, is money, anyway?

In Africa, money has included cowrie shells, metal rings called manillas, coins minted by sultanates on the eastern coast. But people have also traded things of real value: crops, cooking pots, cows. Even today in many parts of Africa, cows are a measure of wealth, like giant cud-chewing coins.

But in the late 1800s, the empires of Europe were busy carving out colonies, and they had a problem: They needed their colonies to make money — the kind they could take back home. But who in their right mind wanted give up their way of life to work for scraps of paper and metal? No one.

To solve this problem, the German colonists in what is now Tanzania (as in other places) introduced taxes that had to be paid in hard currency. Tax resisters (and those who refused to grow the right crops) were jailed or beaten and their villages burned. These policies caused uprisings including the 1905 Maji Maji Rebellion, to which the colonists responded with a scorched-earth "famine policy" that killed as many as 300,000 people. After that, residents paid taxes, though as one missionary complained, "as soon as people have paid the least of their property tax, the desire for money comes to an end for the most part."

A century later, that is no longer the case. Money has sunk deep roots, and only a few groups remain more or less outside the cash economy: the Maasai, the Barabaig, the Hadza. Otherwise Tanzania, like every country, is part of the global monetary system, in which some currencies are more equal than others.

Knowing this history doesn't make our relationship with money any less complicated. I still had to figure out who to employ and what I could afford. If I didn't hire anyone, I risked being seen as a miser (*mchoyo*) who liked to sit alone inside on my piles of money. There were few worse things to be called.

If I wanted to last the year on my savings, I could afford to hire someone to do laundry and someone to clean my house once a week, and to help pay the cook at another volunteer's house where I ate lunch. At first I felt guilty, but eventually I came to see that guilt was not useful. It often led to emotional responses to problems far beyond the scope of the individual: One person cannot redistribute the world's wealth.

But the other thing I came to realize was that I was suffering from a silent affliction — or an affliction of silence. Having to think so much about money made me realize that, in my culture, we never talk money. Like politics and religion, it is taboo. We worry over whether we deserve it, or have earned it, or want more of it. It is something that divides us, so we like to pretend it doesn't exist.

This wasn't the case in Tanzania. When my student called me a rich man, he was stating a fact. When people said America was a rich country, they were not issuing a moral judgment. Gradually, I became more comfortable talking about money. People asked how much I had, and I told them. People asked how much I made, and I told them. Likewise, I could ask others how much they made, and they were happy to share. Eventually it became one of my favorite topics. It was one that interested everybody. It opened doors. It allowed for cross-cultural exchange.

When my student said I was a rich man, I could tell him how rich — and also how expensive it was to live in America. I could tell him that, no, the government in America doesn't give everyone a house, and most people don't have 12 cars. I could tell him that, yes, life was good there, but you also had to work hard, and you rarely had time to sit for an hour with a neighbor, sipping tea. I watched his eyes grow wider as he added up all the monthly expenses.

At the same time, I got a look into how the country I was living in worked: how much a teacher made, a milk seller, a mechanic — how much it cost for a taxi driver to rent his taxi, or to build a mud house, or to put on a wedding, or to buy a bag of cement.

This transformed how I saw the country— the hardship, the struggle, the success, and the failure. It helped me to know that not everyone who asked for help needed it, and not everyone who needed it asked. It let real relationships develop in spite of the divide between the economies we came from. And it helped put my own relative wealth in perspective. I left the country much richer than I'd arrived.

April 2013

Strange trips: On culture and illness

Over the years, I have regurgitated my share of dodgy dishes eaten on the road. I had my appendix removed in a Tanzanian hospital. I watched helplessly, imagining the discovery of my shriveled corpse, as my blood pooled on the floor of a guesthouse room in Borneo after I pulled a leech off my ankle. I know that the last place you want to end up while traveling is in the hospital.

Yet apart from the usual bodily afflictions that come with travel, even stranger maladies prey on our minds when we are abroad. Less well understood than their bacterial counterparts, these are what some scientists call "traveling pathologies." I first came across them while researching cultural syndromes for my book, *The Geography of Madness.*

Cultural syndromes are things like *ode ori*, a condition found among the Yoruba people in Nigeria in which sufferers feel as though something is crawling through their head or another part of their body. In Japan, young people with *hikikomori* refuse to leave their rooms for years and cannot draw the face of their mother. In Bikaner, in northern India, people who come down with Gilhari syndrome feel as though a lizard has lodged itself under their skin and is slowly making its way toward their windpipe.

The list is long and colorful and controversial. Some Western scientists consider these to be local versions of universal conditions. Other people, including me, think they are inextricable from the place from which they emerge — that they are caused by an interaction between culture and biology. That's why Americans have panic attacks with palpitations, tingling, trembling, and fear of "going crazy," while Cambodians have "wind attacks," a fear that the blood vessels in their neck will explode from accumulating too much wind. Both are related to anxiety. Both are shaped by culture.

In the 1970s and '80s, an Italian psychiatrist named Graziella Magherini began to make note of tourists who came to Florence and, while viewing great works of art, experienced a mental breakdown. Often, they had to be put on a stretcher and taken to a psychiatric hospital. Magherini looked at 106 such cases and labeled the condition "Stendhal syndrome," after the French novelist who described having such an experience in a Florence basilica. Russian writer Fyodor Dostoevsky may have had a similar affliction.

According to Magherini, such a breakdown is caused by the power of art over people who are psychologically vulnerable, or by "coming into contact with great works of art without the mediation of a professional guide," as one paper on the syndrome described it. That may be the case. But such experiences are not unique to Italy, regardless of the power of its art. Rather, I suspect there was a greater power at work, one the victims brought with them: the power of their own expectations.

A similar condition has affected some Japanese tourists in Paris. Researchers observed that in Japan, "Paris has, and holds, a quasi-magical power of attraction because the city is considered a symbol of European culture." Besides the normal stresses of travel and the vast cultural differences, the authors noted that "disappointment linked to contact with the everyday reality [of Paris] is a factor of incomprehension and anxiety, but also of disenchantment and depression." This was dubbed "Paris syndrome" by the media.

Paris syndrome is often mentioned in connection with Jerusalem syndrome, in which some visitors to the holy city have a psychotic break and are overcome by "the need to scream, shout, or sing out loud psalms, verses from the Bible, religious hymns, or spirituals." Others channel characters from the Bible. Some of these people have preexisting psychiatric conditions, but many do not. These latter types "possess an idealistic subconscious image of Jerusalem [and] … are unable to deal with the concrete reality of Jerusalem today." Researchers consider the outbursts "an attempt to bridge the gap between these two representations of Jerusalem."

In China in the 1990s, another traveling pathology was noted among passengers who rode overcrowded trains across the country and who sometimes began to hallucinate and attack fellow riders. Psychiatrists called this *lutu jingshenbing* or "traveling psychosis." Continental Europe in the 19th century saw patients who entered a "fugue," wandering sometimes hundreds of miles with no memory of where they had been. Cases multiplied after a Frenchman named Jean-Albert Dadas was diagnosed with the disorder in 1886, but they later died down.

Like cultural syndromes, traveling pathologies are not simple biochemical breakdowns. Rather, they are the result of many factors, including a mix of our experience and our belief about it. They emerge from the space between our hopes and our reality, between the experience we expected and the one we actually have. Sometimes, for some people, that gulf is too great.

Cultural syndromes operate on the same principles: We all have a certain understanding of how things are supposed to go, about the possible chains of events stretching out into the future. If *this*, then *that*. Our world is built on presumed cause and effect, on carefully ordered stories from our so-called cultural scripts.

These teach us not only what happens, but why. Between the events, we see the cause, be it chemistry or God or wind or luck. We believe in these things, and our beliefs affect us in powerful ways. When they're not making us, they can break us.

That's why when I travel, even though I am wary of malaria and E. coli and organ failure, this other fear also lurks. Our own culture is often invisible until we leave it and find ourselves grasping for a rope. If I go to Cambodia, I can't come down with a wind attack, because we are immune from the syndromes of other cultures. But I know I can never be immune from my own. Wherever you go, you bring a world with you.

May 2016

The pursuit of unhappiness: On sadness and growth

Last year, when the new Dostoevsky subway station opened in Moscow, there was worried speculation that the grim scenes from Dostoevsky's novels, artistically depicted on the gray marble walls (*Crime and Punishment*'s Raskolnikov about to murder the old woman with an axe, the troubled protagonist of *Demons* holding a gun to his head), were so depressing that people, overwhelmed by the bleakness, would start throwing themselves onto the tracks.

Fortunately, the feared rash of suicides has not materialized. This could be because people don't make those kinds of decisions based on subway art. Or it could be because Russians have a different attitude about happiness than Americans do. According to one recent study, they tend to have darker, more negative thoughts. But they also worry less about those feelings, and thus experience fewer depressive symptoms than Americans. Russians may brood more, but they don't dwell that much on their brooding. Americans, meanwhile, brood about their worrying and end up more depressed than the Russians.

It is, perhaps, a simple fact of American life: We expect to be happy. The right to pursue happiness is part of the Declaration of Independence, after all. The feeling has been heightened of late by the booming field of "happiness studies," which has produced a flow of news stories and books about what will and won't make us happy, about the happiest places to live, and about how to structure our lives so we can be happy almost all the time.

Some important findings have emerged. Too many choices lead to dissatisfaction. Chronic pain has a more negative impact than a single accident. We habituate quickly to our acquisitions. A good marriage is worth about $100,000 a year in terms of how happy it makes us.

But this headlong rush toward happiness might ultimately backfire. Could our constant worrying about why we are not happy be making us more miserable than if we simply accepted some occasional unhappiness as part of life? In viewing unhappiness as a problem to be solved, might we not miss what a little sadness has to offer us? Are we trading long-term satisfaction for feeling good right now? Purchasing our present-day enjoyment at the cost of future meaning?

Children are a case in point. Recently, there has been a spate of news stories stating that having children does not increase one's happiness by any objective measure. In fact, marital satisfaction declines steeply when kids are born and doesn't recover until they leave. As researcher Daniel Gilbert says, the only symptom of "empty-nest syndrome" is smiling.

Having two young children myself, I can more or less confirm this is true. And yet, despite all the headaches, sleep deprivation, stained furniture, and general crabbiness, few parents I know regret their decision. One study even found that mothers ages 36 to 44 were less likely to be depressed than their childless peers, even if, at a given point on a given day, they may be less happy. Raising kids isn't nonstop fun. But eventually (we hope) we'll be better for it.

This jibes with the conclusions of some earlier research. In the 1980s, psychologist Mihaly Csikszentmihalyi found that people did not report their most satisfying experiences as relaxing on the beach, or going to parties, or finally buying that car they'd always wanted. The happy moments came when they were working hard at something, moving toward some goal they had, being challenged and absorbed and focused. A more recent investigation from the *Journal of Happiness Studies* also found that people who were working hard to accomplish something felt more stress in the moment but were happier in the long term.

Suffering is no fun, and we usually try to avoid it. But it is also inevitable. Not so long ago, when life was less certain and comfortable, people understood that suffering could be an opportunity to rise to a challenge. They were willing to at least try to extract some meaning from it.

When I lived abroad, I went through what's known as culture shock. Culture shock is not, as many people think, the confusion you experience in a foreign fruit market as you calculate kilos to pounds or pesos to dollars. Rather, it's a series of mood swings that occur as you learn to function in another culture. As anyone who has gone through this can attest, it can be a dark time.

But as you find ways to cope, you become a new person — someone stronger, more capable, more aware. As you struggle with culture shock, or any of life's difficulties, something remarkable happens: You grow.

For a while, I didn't understand this. I couldn't fathom why I had developed an odd nostalgia for a time that I remembered as a hard and deeply unhappy one. But that was precisely the time when I stopped being the person I had been and started becoming the person I am. Now, when I recall those unhappy days, I think of them as the best days of my life.

May 2011

At arm's length: On elbow room

Some years ago, my wife and I went to the south of Thailand to teach English at an elementary school. It was a poor school in a small town. The principal did his best to accommodate us, building a room for us to live in at the school. It had a bathroom and a shower and many, many photos of the school's owner. By local standards it was luxurious.

By our standards, however, it was missing one main thing: privacy. A buffer zone between ourselves and everyone else. The room was situated right next to the principal's office, and our shared wall stopped about a foot short of the ceiling. Our bed sat against one side of this wall. On the other side was the principal's desk. It felt, in a way, as though we were in bed with him.

This was not the first time I had noticed cultural differences regarding personal space. When I lived in East Africa, I saw how my need for space seemed strange and possibly hostile in a very people-oriented culture. But Americans have long been notorious for the vast expanses of personal space we need. An article titled "Understanding American Culture" on the International Student Guide to the USA website advises: "Americans tend to require more personal space than in other cultures. If you try to get too close to an American during your conversation, he or she will feel that you are 'in their face' and will try to back away. Try to avoid physical contact while you are speaking, since this may lead to discomfort."

For me, being touched during a conversation does, in fact, lead to discomfort, as does sitting unnecessarily close to my compatriots. Whenever I get on a bus or sit in a theater, I look around, take in the distances between people, and triangulate to find the seat that is as far as possible from everyone. Anthropologist Edward Hall, who coined the term "proxemics" to describe the ways humans use space, argued that this tendency stems from the fact that America is a "non-contact culture," like some others in Asia, northern Europe, and Britain. A characteristic of those cultures is an aversion to being touched by strangers.

Americans, Hall found, reserve the space up to 18 inches away from ourselves for intimate contact; the space from 18 inches to 4 feet away is our "personal distance," appropriate for good friends or family members; and we relegate our acquaintances to an area 4 to 10 feet from us (our "social distance"). Our "public distance" is about 10 feet. If the seats on the bus were each 10 feet apart, we would all be very happy.

Hall contrasted us with "contact cultures" like those found in the Arab world, southern Europe, and much of Africa, where people stand closer, touch more, and hold eye contact longer. In Europe generally, he found, people preferred a conversational distance of 2 to 3 feet.

More recent studies have shown how personal space can also vary according to who people are conversing with and even what language they are using. In Iran, ethnic Kurdish and Mazandarani women had an average personal distance of about 3 feet with women from their own ethnic group. But with women from other groups, the Mazandarani women's personal space dropped to 2.4 feet, while the Kurdish women pushed their boundary out to almost 4 feet.

Another study looked at American, Japanese, and Venezuelan students at a Midwestern university and found that when speaking Spanish, Venezuelans sat 32 inches apart, but when speaking English, they sat 40 inches apart. The Japanese students, whose preferred interpersonal space was 5 inches greater than either of the other groups, actually moved slightly closer to each other when speaking English (38.5 inches) than they did when speaking Japanese (40 inches).

Where does our American need for space come from? Is it a remnant of our country's frontier mentality? An inheritance from our cool northern European forebears? A vestige of our tradition of extreme individualism? Whatever the case, it runs deep in our culture, as evidenced by the long-popular dream to escape the crowd, to go off the grid, to retreat to a cabin in the woods.

"To be in company, even with the best," wrote Henry David Thoreau in *Walden*, "is soon wearisome and dissipating. I love to be alone. I never found the companion as companionable as solitude."

Like Thoreau, I prefer spending vast stretches of time alone. Yet as our society has become more prosperous and our technology has advanced, our ability to keep others at a distance has grown, and I've begun to wonder about how our hunger for space vies with our need for company.

Some researchers have grown alarmed at rising rates of loneliness: In 1985, the most common answer to the question, "How many confidants do you have?" was "three." But in 2004, the most common answer was "none" — given by 25 percent of respondents. And if you exclude family members, that figure jumped to 50 percent.

Solitude and loneliness are different things. Solitude is simply being alone with oneself. Loneliness stems from a lack of a desired social connection. If your relationships are superficial, or you feel misunderstood, this, too, can create a feeling of loneliness. (As Thoreau also said, "We are for the most part more lonely when we go abroad among men than when we stay in our chambers.") Solitude is something you can choose. Loneliness is not.

According to psychologist John Cacioppo, author of *Loneliness: Human Nature and the Need for Social Connection*, the feeling is "an alarm signal, embedded in the genes," that warns us to "do something to alter an uncomfortable and potentially dangerous condition." Our physiological response to loneliness is similar to the experience of physical pain.

But while loneliness may have evolved as a warning sign, we now know that it is also a dangerous condition in itself. Loneliness suppresses immune response, raises blood pressure, and can increase the risk of heart attack by 29 percent and stroke by 32 percent. Loneliness can lead to depression, paranoia, and social anxiety. The overall health risk is on par with smoking 15 cigarettes a day. Chronic loneliness can increase overall risk of mortality by 26 percent.

In her book *The Village Effect: How Face-to-Face Contact Can Make Us Healthier, Happier, and Smarter*, psychologist Susan Pinker argues that personal contact is the key to reversing many of those effects. It creates a shield against disease, helping decrease inflammation, improve metabolism, and boost immune response. She makes the case that most of the mental and physical benefits associated with attending church or sharing family meals actually are the result of having meaningful interactions with others on a regular basis.

I still don't want to share a wall with the school principal. But I do worry about the premium our culture puts on personal space. As it becomes easier to fill the gaps in the walls around us, each of us inside our own digital fortress, it's possible to imagine a day when we've managed to create a personal space with only enough room for one.

March 2017

The bicultural advantage: On travel and creativity (Part II)

Years ago, I was eating at McDonald's in a Florence, Italy, train station when I spotted three tall men in American football jerseys. I was glad to see some compatriots, so I went over and struck up a conversation. It turned out that the Americans were playing for a league that was trying to spread the sport in Europe, apparently without much success. We chatted for a while, and one of them mentioned that his contract was almost up.

"Man, I can't wait to get out of here," he said, "and get back to the real world."

I knew exactly what he meant. I'd also experienced the feeling that in this new country, nothing made sense, no rules were obeyed, and the basic logic of the universe didn't apply. But then I'd started speaking the language, understanding the logic, and moving into a space where the Italian world felt more real to me than the American one I'd left behind.

I recalled the football player's remark recently, when I heard about some new research. It seems that living abroad is not simply a matter of relocation. It's a matter of mindset. And what you get out of it depends more on what goes on in your head than on your dates of arrival and departure.

Those of us who have lived abroad know how expatriates fall into archetypes. There's the complainer, the one who sees all that's wrong with the new place, and all that is right with the old one, and who constantly tries to recruit newcomers to his or her point of view. There's the one who's gone native, who sports local attire, marries a local, will only speak the local language (even with fellow expats) and, after returning home, gets in trouble with the health department for butchering a chicken in his apartment. Then there are the rest of us, who end up somewhere in between.

For a long time, I thought these categories were arbitrary, with the main difference being how well a person mastered the local language. But I now know that researchers have developed a more sophisticated understanding of how people deal with life abroad.

Every person has an individual response to the opportunities and stresses of living in a new country. In the academic realm, this is called an "acculturation strategy," and the one you choose depends on many things: your personality, your circumstances, and whether you are an immigrant, a refugee, or a "sojourner," someone who plans to stay for a limited time.

The football player and I were both sojourners, but we found different paths through the maze of Italian culture. His seemed to be what's called "separation," or the rejection of the new culture in favor of the one at home. Meanwhile, I had moved toward "assimilation," or the rejection of one's home culture in favor of the new one.

Eventually, I would swing back toward something closer to "biculturalism," in which you learn the new ways of thinking, speaking, and interacting but retain your old ones. It means having two separate identities — in my case, an Italian one and an American one.

I'm not blaming the football player, or taking credit myself. I was lucky, because I was living with an Italian family, going to an Italian school, and making lots of Italian friends. I was learning to see the world through their eyes. The football player, on the other hand, was living with Americans, playing an American game, and speaking English all the time. It's hard to get immersed in a new culture when you're living in a bubble.

Immersion is difficult (though perhaps no harder than the separation strategy), but it's worth the effort. A team led by Carmit Tador, of Tel Aviv University; Adam Galinsky, a researcher at the Kellogg School of Management at Northwestern University; and William Maddux, of the international business school INSEAD, recently concluded a decade of research that sheds some light on this.

They had already found that living abroad tends to make people more creative. But their latest work shows that biculturalism (versus the other strategies) also makes people more professionally successful, more entrepreneurial, and more innovative at work. Biculturalism, in other words, is good for business.

Why? According to Galinsky, it has to do with "integrative complexity," something of a holy grail in psychology. It means being able to see things from multiple points of view, make connections between them, and integrate them into something new.

That ability to consider and combine perspectives is linked to both creativity and success. In a separate study of the letters of U.S. Civil War generals, which analyzed the writing for density of ideas and perspectives, higher levels of integrative complexity correlated with battlefield success. The study found that Robert E. Lee was more complex than most of the generals he beat, but less complex than the general who beat him, Ulysses S. Grant.

As it turns out, living abroad, and learning to see how things appear through the lens of a different culture, is one way to develop this kind of thinking. "Basically," Galinsky told me, "what we showed is that the act of adapting and integrating your experiences with your host culture leads to these long-term transformations in terms of the complexity of thoughts. And that allows people to be more creative, more entrepreneurial, and have better reputations and higher promotion rates."

This research suggests the importance of exchange programs and of exposure to other cultures. It shows the value of learning languages that give you access to other ways of thinking. It demonstrates the worth of employees who've lived in another country. But it also shows that simply living abroad is not enough.

Complex thinking "is really about two things," Galinsky says. "One is trying to look for differences — looking to see when things are different from your home culture. And second, looking to see why those differences exist. It's not just thinking about the host culture, it's thinking about the host culture in relation to the home culture. It's that comparison process."

When you reach a point where you're straddling two ways of thinking, that's where you begin to see things that others might miss. It is there — between two equally real worlds — that the doors of possibility open.

Maybe that football player was having a bad day. I hope he got to know the real Italy. Maybe it seemed more real to him once he got home. If he learned to see the world through new eyes, there's no telling what paths have opened up before him.

December 2012

CHANGE

The cost of fame: On egos and empathy

Growing up, I spent shocking amounts of time in front of the television. We may have had only 13 channels at our house, but we stared at them, slack-jawed, for hours on end. My mother assured us that our heads were rotting from the inside out.

These days, I don't spend nearly as much time in front of the tube. This is partly because I don't have time, partly because the internet is more interesting, and partly because, at the tender age of 41, I am a prematurely cranky old man, and therefore easily infuriated.

Either TV has changed or I have changed. This dawned on me last year as I was channel-surfing at a hotel, unable to settle on anything — until I came across a rerun of *The Lawrence Welk Show*. I set down the remote and sat happily transfixed till the end. My inner 80-year-old had taken over.

Over the years, people have looked at the "vast wasteland" of television and seen the approaching end of Western civilization. I try to take criticism of the medium with a grain of salt, but I recently came across some studies suggesting that it wasn't only me who had changed.

Two researchers at the University of California, Yalda Uhls and Patricia Greenfield, devised a way to measure the values expressed in U.S. television shows. Their idea was not that TV is a corrupting influence or a source of moral instruction, but a mirror that reflects our society back to us.

Given how much the world has changed over the decades, you might not think that TV shows from the years 1967, 1977, 1987, and 1997 would have much in common. But they did. Taking the two most popular programs for tweens from each of those years, as well as from 2007, Uhls and Greenfield looked for 16 values demonstrated by the characters, such as benevolence, popularity, community feeling, financial success, tradition, and fame.

For the first four decades, the shows were fairly consistent: Community feeling was the top value for all of them except 1987, when it ranked second. Benevolence and tradition were consistently at the top. Meanwhile, fame ranked 15th in 1967, 1987, and 1997. (In 1977, it was 13th.) Achievement and financial success hovered around the bottom half of the list; they were never dominant forces in the characters' lives.

By 2007, however, community feeling had dropped to the 11th spot. Benevolence had fallen to 12th, and tradition to 15th. Financial success had jumped from 12th to 5th since 1997, achievement to 2nd, and fame to 1st.

In the age of *American Idol*, you might have expected as much — and the researchers did, in fact, anticipate that individualist values would have moved upward. But they were surprised by the magnitude of the change. "If you believe that television reflects the culture, as I do," Uhls says, "then American culture has changed drastically."

There are a slew of related trends. Narcissism has been rising for several decades. In the early 1950s, only 12 percent of teens ages 14-16 agreed with the statement "I am an important person." By the late 1980s, 80 percent did. In a study that ran from 1979 to 2006, scores on the Narcissistic Personality Inventory rose by 30 percent among college students. By 2006, the average college student scored nearly the same level of narcissism as the average celebrity. Researcher Jean Twenge says we are seeing an epidemic, which she details in her 2009 book, *The Narcissism Epidemic: Living in the Age of Entitlement.*

We are also seeing decreases in empathy. One study found that from 1979 to 2009, college students' "empathetic concern" (the capacity to feel what others are feeling) dropped 48 percent, and their "perspective taking" (the ability to see from another's point of view) declined by 34 percent. Psychologist Sara Konrath summed this up as an "empathy paradox," in which we are finding "increasing disconnection in the age of connection."

Researchers have suggested several possible causes. Smaller family size is one, as is the decline of social organizations, which Robert Putnam wrote about in his 2001 book *Bowling Alone: The Collapse and Revival of American Community*. The internet and social media play a role; many of the changes accelerated after 2000. But Konrath points out that these trends started several decades ago. After all, Tom Wolfe called the 1970s the "Me Decade," arguing that a great religious awakening had occurred, centered on the worship of the self.

Another cause may be the self-esteem movement of the 1980s — which, research shows, did little good. Much of what still passes for self-esteem building, Twenge argues, fosters self-importance and narcissism. Self-esteem is the result of accomplishment, not the cause of it. High self-esteem doesn't lead to academic achievement, or good behavior, or less violence or drug use. What the self-esteem movement has led to is grade inflation — 30 percent more students getting As, even as SAT scores are declining. "After all these years," psychologist Roy Baumeister wrote in 2005, "my recommendation is this: Forget about self-esteem and concentrate more on self-control and self-discipline."

What do these changes mean, and what are the implications for our society? Will our egos keep growing? Will they swing back to some historical norm? Will people eventually rebel against the narcissistic tide?

We are still mapping out the extent of the transformation. But one of the costs may be our very sense of well-being. We are social animals; we need to take part in others' lives, and have them take part in ours. Many researchers suggest that our rising levels of stress, anxiety, and depression stem from rising levels of self-regard. The negative health effects of loneliness are well-documented, as are the health benefits of being socially engaged. Konrath and her colleagues found that people who did volunteer work had a lower mortality risk four years later. The more regularly and frequently they volunteered, the lower the risk. But this was only true if the person volunteered for other-oriented reasons. Among those who volunteered for selfish reasons, the mortality rate was the same as that of non-volunteers.

What's best for society may also be what's best for ourselves.

June 2013

Dinner for one: On meals and mores

There is a new ritual in American life. It goes like this: Whenever you invite someone to dinner, you must inquire about any special dietary needs. Because today, it seems that nearly everyone has drawn a line around foods that cannot pass their lips.

This could be because of allergies, moral qualms, lifestyle choices, health issues, or simple preference. The person might be a vegetarian who eats fish, a carnivore who hates carbs, a glutton who avoids gluten, or a time bomb waiting to be set off by a nut. (Asking ahead makes for a more pleasant evening than calling an ambulance.)

Hospitalization aside, one reason for this shift has been the moralization of food. Our dining choices have become identity choices, a way of saying, "This is the kind of person I am," or "This is the kind of world I want to live in."

This is a luxury of our age. The hunters, villagers, and small bands of Homo sapiens in times past would have thought it extremely strange, and possibly hostile, to assert one's preferences in this manner.

When I went to live in Tanzania, I was a 24-year-old eco-minded vegetarian. In the cafeteria of a liberal arts college, that was one thing. But whenever I tried to explain my beliefs about the earth and responsible use of resources to Tanzanian neighbors who invited me into their homes, I felt silly and self-indulgent. My preferences didn't seem to have anything to do with the chicken set down in front of me. Soon I began to feel that the generosity I was being shown was worth more than this idea I had brought with me. Rejecting their food was a rejection of the people, of their company, of our relationship. In Tanzania, the worst thing you could be called was *mchoyo*, or selfish. Meals were meant to be shared, and one of the worst fates was to eat alone.

For much of humanity's time on the planet, this has been the norm: People gathered around the carcass and ate together. Sharing food was how the group survived, and over time, it came to be one of our core ways of interacting with one another, of building our community. "Eating together," writes French sociologist Claude Fischler in his 2015 book *Selective Eating: The Rise, Meaning and Sense of Personal Dietary Requirements*, "is seen as bringing people together, and … eating the same thing … means symbolically building or rebuilding a common destiny."

Sharing food is a way of saying, "This is who we are."

Sharing food at a table makes us part of something bigger than ourselves. Researchers who have looked at the effects of family meals on children have found that when adolescents eat with their families on a regular basis, they are at lower risk for alcohol abuse, violent behavior, eating disorders, poor academic performance, and mental illnesses such as depression.

But America has always been a highly individualized culture, and as the demand for special food shows, this fragmentation is accelerating. In the past, refusing food offered by a host would have been seen as an indication of dislike or distrust. Yet today it happens all too frequently. A decade ago, when American journalist Pamela Druckerman moved to France (where the special meal craze still has not caught on), she was a vegetarian on a low-carb diet. But when she went to friends' houses, they expected her to eat what they had prepared. No one cared about her dietary preferences.

The French are famously proud of their way of dining, which is included on UNESCO's Intangible Cultural Heritage of Humanity list and remains strikingly formal: In 2010, the average French person spent 2 hours and 10 minutes at meals each day. This is partly because the French idea of food is different from ours. Americans tend of think of food as fuel, as nutrition; the same report found that people in the United States spend only 1 hour and 3 minutes a day eating and drinking. But when French people are asked what "eating well" means, they talk about eating good food in moderate amounts with a *convive* — someone with whom you share a meal. In France, 80 percent of meals are eaten with others.

In Great Britain a few years ago, a minor panic ensued when a national survey found that 65 percent of people rarely if ever hosted dinner parties because they were too stressful, too expensive, or too time-consuming. A similar trend has been seen in the United States, where the percentage of people who had spent a social evening with their neighbors more than once a month dropped from 44 in 1974 to 30 in 2008. Meanwhile, the *Washington Post* reports that in the U.S., we eat nearly half of all meals and snacks alone, and 65 percent of us either eat lunch at our desks or skip it altogether.

Is the dinner party doomed? And what would that mean for our society? In her book *Reclaiming Conversation: The Power of Talk in a Digital Age*, psychologist Sherry Turkle says we are experiencing a "flight from conversation," in which our main goal is to avoid talking to one another. "We once taught our children to ignore a ringing phone at dinner," she writes. "We became annoyed if telemarketers interrupted us. Now, Facebook suggests that it may be a good thing to interrupt dinner ourselves."

Sometimes it does seem as if we are headed down a path leading far from Tanzania, far from France, to a place where we each have our own perfectly crafted meals that we eat in our own soundproof bubbles.

Hoping for encouragement, I called Rico Gagliano and Brendan Francis Newnam, hosts of the radio show *The Dinner Party Download*. They acknowledge the forces working against the dinner party: the foodie arms race, our overscheduled lives, cellphones, cat videos, brunch. And yet, they argue, gathering around a table continues to be important — even if there are special orders for every belief and immune system, even if we are not all symbolically building a common destiny.

And it doesn't have anything to do with the food or the cloth napkins or the presentation.

"Food is essential for a dinner party," Gagliano says. "But it's not the most important part."

It's about the company, the conversation, the *convives*. Sharing a meal — whether at home, in a restaurant, or on a blanket in the park — is about creating a place where you can talk and ask questions and be curious and learn who people are.

"We would have a better society if we had more dinner parties," says Newnam. "The dinner party is the space where you should be able to talk about everything. Where else are you going to have those kinds of exchanges if not over a table with food and wine?"

April 2016

It's only human: On dehumanization and cyclists

One day recently, I was driving down a narrow street near my home. In front of me, two cyclists were taking up most of the lane, going — as cyclists tend to do — well below the speed limit. As we rolled along, I got angrier and angrier. Why didn't they get on the bike path next to the road? Why didn't they move over a little so we could pass? *Who were these people?*

Eventually I got around them and cooled off. But I was surprised by my reaction. After all, I'm a cyclist myself, and I have been on the receiving end of drivers' abuse. But at that moment, I did not see myself in those riders. I couldn't imagine what was going on in their heads. They were like an alien species on two wheels. It was as if I had drawn a line between people like me and people like them.

This is a thought process known as "dehumanization," which sounds like something that only happens at Nazi death camps, in Cambodian killing fields, or at roadblocks in Rwanda. But in fact, we draw these kinds of lines every day, often without any idea that we're doing it.

Nick Haslam, a professor of psychology at the University of Melbourne in Australia, is one of the leading thinkers on dehumanization. To measure how drivers dehumanize cyclists, Haslam and his colleagues surveyed more than 400 people. In one typical result, 55 percent of noncyclists saw cyclists as "less than 100 percent human." (So did 30 percent of cyclists.)

"Some drivers are more willing than others to say that cyclists are more primitive, less evolved, or more animal-like than other people," Haslam says.

In the early days of research into dehumanization, in an effort to understand how people are able to do horrible things to other people, much of the focus was on ethnic groups. More recent research has shown that dehumanizing attitudes can be aimed at anyone: women, medical patients, immigrants, the mentally ill, homeless people.

Researchers have also established that dehumanization is not an all-or-nothing prospect. There are degrees, even kinds, of dehumanization. What Haslam calls "animalistic" dehumanization is the feeling that members of another group are not as human as we are. We see them as having basic emotions such as joy, anger, fear, and surprise — but not more complicated ones such as pride, admiration, and remorse. We see them as lacking "human essence," or as being a kind of animal that needs to be overseen by those of us who are more evolved.

In Haslam's model, the second major form of dehumanization is called "mechanistic" dehumanization, in which we see people as lacking not merely human essence, but human nature itself. We see them not as a lesser version of us, but as something completely different, like a machine or a robot or an empty vessel acting out of cold self-interest.

When we draw these lines between ourselves and others, sometimes we draw them lightly; other times we construct them like an impenetrable wall. It's as if we had an internal dimmer switch for turning down the humanity of others. The further it is turned down, the harder it is to imagine the minds or hearts of those people. Haslam says there are many reasons we do this. "Sometimes we dehumanize people to make it easier to harm them, but I don't think this is the most common reason," he says. "More often it is just one aspect of a general human tendency to favor the groups we belong to over other groups. People tend to see their 'in-group' as better and more human than 'out-groups.' This may serve an evolved function of promoting strong ties with one's group."

In the mists of time, this propensity to see our own group as more human than others would have had survival benefits to a small tribe trying to survive in a hostile world. We don't live in small tribes anymore, but part of us still wants to find the border of our group, to defend it, to see those inside it as more human than those outside it — even if we know intellectually that this is not the case.

Our ability to dehumanize runs so deep that it can be observed in our brains. In 2006, Princeton University scientists Susan Fiske and Lasana Harris published a study in which they put 22 students into a functional magnetic resonance imaging (fMRI) machine, which allowed them to view blood flow to, and activation of, parts of the brain. While the students were in the imager, they were shown either objects or photos of people who appear to fit certain social stereotypes, such as middle-class, rich, elderly, disabled, and homeless.

Most of the photos activated the parts of the brain we use for social cognition. This is what happens when we think about another person. But two groups — homeless people and drug addicts — triggered no activation. They were not being perceived as human.

Fiske had anticipated this. She had been developing a theory of dehumanization called the Stereotype Content Model, in which there are two criteria by which we measure people we meet: warmth and competence. "What do you need to know about people who are unfamiliar to you?" she says. "First you need to know their intentions — good or ill. If their intentions are benign, you trust them more. If they're malignant, you don't. Then you need to know whether they can act on their intentions. Because if they can't act on their intentions, they don't really matter to you. That's competence."

These two measures form a square with four quadrants into which we sort the people we meet. Those we consider to be like us are both warm and competent. People we envy are those we see as competent but not warm (think Wall Street bankers). We see people we pity or sympathize with as warm but not competent (disabled or elderly people). And people who are neither competent nor warm we see as something else entirely.

Fiske's groups correspond roughly to Haslam's mechanistic dehumanization (cold/competent) and animalistic dehumanization (warm/incompetent). But she adds a category for the more fully dehumanized group about whom we feel nothing but disgust.

This landscape of lines we draw between ourselves and others is far from simple, but researchers are starting to map it out. The next step is to figure out how to blur the lines or erase them, and thereby expand the circle of humanity. To rehumanize people.

Some of this work was done in the 20th century with the rise of internationalism, out of which grew Rotary, along with the United Nations, the Red Cross, and other organizations urging an expanded understanding of humanity. As Article 1 of the Universal Declaration of Human Rights states: "All human beings are born free and equal in dignity and rights. They are endowed with reason and conscience and should act towards one another in a spirit of brotherhood." We aspire to this, even if we don't always practice it. And we have come a long way since the world of small, struggling tribes. But there is always more progress to be made.

Fiske has found one method of reversing dehumanization. The idea behind it is simple: to force yourself to see things from the other person's perspective. To do this, she conducted a study in which she simply asked subjects in the imaging machine whether the dehumanized person likes to eat a particular vegetable. This strange question had a profound effect: The social cognition areas of the brain lit up again. It turns out you can't imagine what someone likes without seeing them as a person.

"If you think about what's going on inside someone's head," Fiske says, "they become a human being again."

September 2018

Frankenwords: On jargon and meaninglessness

I don't remember exactly when the menu at Starbucks started bothering me, but it must have been almost the first time I stepped into one. It wasn't the range of products or the drinks themselves — which I enjoyed. It was the names of three coffee sizes: *tall, grande,* and *venti,* otherwise known as "small, medium, and large."

For years I engaged in a kind of guerrilla campaign of not using them.

"I'll take a large, please."

"Venti?"

"Yes, large, thank you."

This was petty and annoying, I know, but I couldn't help myself. I wasn't even sure why it irked me, until I realized it was something quite simple: a flagrant disregard for meaning, the notion that you can take a word and bend it to your own purposes. To make a *small* into a *tall* felt like a glimpse of a world where people could buy a word, gut it, then fill it with whatever they wanted. Language is an agreement, a social contract. This felt like a violation.

Changing the word doesn't change the thing it describes. It only creates a wider gulf between rhetoric and reality. Using the Italian word for large (*grande*) doesn't make a cup any bigger. And calling another one a "venti" doesn't make it anything but the largest of the three drinks on the menu. By historical standards, they all contain large amounts of coffee. But we are not ordering historically. We are ordering comparatively.

These may seem like small concerns. But I can't help feeling they are a bellwether of some broader change. In his essay "Politics and the English Language," George Orwell lamented the creep of clichés and jargon into politicians' speeches whenever they didn't want people to understand what they were saying (or didn't themselves know what they meant). Their words hid their meaning instead of clarifying it.

"When there is a gap between one's real and one's declared aims, one turns as it were instinctively to long words and exhausted idioms, like a cuttlefish squirting out ink," Orwell wrote. He was worried that people might dismiss his concerns as sentimental, and I share his fear. Who cares about the Starbucks menu? Big deal. Yet there is reason for concern. We are so inundated with meaningless words that we have grown numb to them.

Recently, I sat down in a coffee shop and overheard a young woman tell a friend that she needed to do some "concepting." (Meaning, I assumed, coming up with some ideas.) In some work environments, entire meetings are conducted in this innovative language, which often contains three or four times the volume of words necessary. In which "I'm noticing you have a gap with your arrival time" means "You're late." Or "Why don't you frame up this project for me" means "Explain this project." Other Orwellian examples include things like "deep dive," "low-hanging fruit," and "continuous improvement," which is neither continuous nor an improvement.

Perhaps the most egregious offenders are in the field of marketing, and one of the most shameless practitioners is David Shing, a self-styled "digital prophet" (an abuse of both words) who calls himself "Shingy" and who strikes me with a nameless terror. With astonishing ease, he separates words from their meaning, coining terms and phrases as he breathes. "I grew up in the age of information," he says in one video. "We are now currently in the middle of the age of social. As you know, fundamentally it's changed, but where it's headed is the world of context or interest ..." The head spins as it grasps for meaning. He's like a living Starbucks menu. (Translation: "He's not showing up in the sense-making space.")

This is the vein that satirists Henry Beard and Christopher Cerf mine in their recent book, *Spinglish: The Definitive Dictionary of Deliberately Deceptive Language*, a long list of words that have been intentionally drained of meaning in order to obfuscate the things they purport to describe.

Three decades ago, the Soviet Union sent "bio-robots" (humans) to clean up Chernobyl. More recently, surveillance has become "data collection." People who are drunk are "overrefreshed." Shredding sensitive papers is "document management." Failure is "deferred success." A dishwasher is a "utensil maintenance professional." A butcher is a "meat technologist." (Either can be "dehired," "decruited," or "deinstalled" at any time.) A profit is a "negative deficit" and a revenue decline is "negative growth," while losses are "deficit enhancement." (That is, assuming no "data massage" has taken place.)

Death is "failure to fulfill one's wellness potential."

A small is a "tall."

Beard and Cerf try to distinguish everyday jargon from deliberately deceptive words. But Orwell made no such distinction. To him they sprang from the same well: a carelessness about, or even a hostility to, the meaning of words.

"A scrupulous writer," Orwell wrote, "in every sentence that he writes, will ask himself at least four questions, thus: What am I trying to say? What words will express it? What image or idiom will make it clearer? Is this image fresh enough to have an effect?"

The alternative is "simply throwing your mind open and letting the ready-made phrases come crowding in. They will construct your sentences for you — even think your thoughts for you, to a certain extent — and at need they will perform the important service of partially concealing your meaning even from yourself."

These concerns may not be new. But today, words flow freely across our screens, via our blogs and tweets and posts and likes. That increased speed may be why the distance we have traveled since Orwell's time seems so great, and why I find it so alarming. We have arrived at a place where images have unrivaled power, where surfaces obscure everything underneath, where we value branding far more than understanding. As writer Daniel Pink has observed, we are all in sales. We are all small, trying to tell the world we are tall.

This feels exhausting. It's always better to see things clearly. And the solution hasn't changed since Orwell: "What is above all needed," he wrote, "is to let the meaning choose the word, not the other way around."

January 2016

On not being Scrooge: On compassion

Down the road in front of me, the light turned red. As our car slowed, from the corner of my eye I saw a man standing in the middle of the street with a sign that said he was homeless and needed money. My wife and two daughters were in the car with me. I looked straight ahead.

From behind me, a small voice spoke. "Can we give him some money?" It was my eight-year-old daughter. I didn't answer. The light turned green, and I drove on. The voice spoke again.

"Why are you so mean, Daddy?" she said.

"Yeah," my wife chimed in, smiling. "Why are you so mean?" She was sort of joking, sort of not. My daughter continued: "How would you feel if you were a poor person and all you had was scraggly clothes and people just drove past you?"

"I don't know," I said. And honestly, I didn't know how I would feel — let alone how that guy felt. In fact, I hadn't thought about that sort of thing for some time. Back in college, for a senior project about homelessness, I'd played a homeless person in a movie. And I'd done some volunteering here and there, but in raising children lately, everything extraneous has been swept away.

For most of the year, it's easy to get absorbed in our own lives. But the holidays are supposed to be different. This is the time when our thoughts are supposed to turn to others — to the people we buy gifts for, to those less fortunate than us. Charles Dickens' *A Christmas Carol* plays on stages across the country. Every year, ghosts visit Ebenezer Scrooge and show him how hard his heart has become, and how little happiness all his wealth has brought him.

Wealth, in itself, is not a bad thing. It often helps you live longer and be healthier. It provides opportunities to see the world. It can fund an education and a place to live. But there can be a cost to having it as well, which research is now untangling. Paul Piff, a psychologist at the University of California, Berkeley, has co-published several studies that have found that wealthy individuals behave less "prosocially" than poorer ones. They give less of their money, percentage-wise, to charity. They feel less compassionate toward people in need. They are more likely to cheat on games (in a laboratory situation). And they are less attuned to the emotional states of others.

All of this seems to suggest, as F. Scott Fitzgerald once wrote, that the very rich are different from you and me (and not just because they have more money, as Ernest Hemingway quipped). But according to Piff, it's not that they are different, it's that being rich makes you different.

In studies that have temporarily altered the self-perceptions of low-income participants, making them feel better off, he says, "suddenly they start behaving as if they are actually wealthy. It's not so much about wealthy people behaving in particular ways, but rather the experience of wealth making people behave in particular ways."

But other research further complicates the subject. One "lost letter" study in London (in which letters were dropped to see how many people would mail them) showed that 87 percent of letters dropped in wealthier neighborhoods were mailed, while only 37 percent were mailed in poorer ones. And though that could be interpreted as looking out for one's own, a Georgetown University study found that altruistic kidney donations (giving a kidney to a stranger) are more likely to take place in wealthy communities than poor ones, a finding that "paradoxically indicates that community-level income may positively predict prosociality even while individual-level wealth does not," the authors wrote.

This is all complex — we humans, after all, are not so easy to figure out. But we may find a key in a 2012 study by the *Chronicle of Philanthropy*, which showed that when wealthy people live in more economically diverse ZIP codes, their charitable giving rises from an average of 2.8 percent to 4.2 percent.

Wealth isolates. Big houses. Big cars. No need to ask favors of people. Perhaps this is what underlies much of the shift in behavior among wealthy individuals. When we don't need to interact with others, our ability to imagine their lives diminishes. Yet this is something Piff says we can easily reverse.

"In our lab work," he says, "we find that wealthy people are less generous in general. But if you show them a brief video about child poverty around the world, they become just as generous as everyone else. So even brief reminders of the needs of others can build an inroad into this psychological island that you inhabit."

As a freelance writer, I've never been what you'd call wealthy. But when I was growing up, my dad was a doctor, and we never worried about where our next meal would come from. Today I live in a neighborhood that is solidly middle class and diverse — in the color of the hybrid cars, if nothing else.

Am I living on an island? And could that be affecting my ability to see the plight of the guy in scraggly clothes? I'd always thought of myself more along the lines of Bob Cratchit. Now I had a miniature Jacob Marley in my back seat, calling me Scrooge.

I don't want to be like that. I don't want to suffer from what the writer George Saunders said was the thing in life he regretted most: failures of kindness. Maybe if it wasn't too late for Scrooge, it wasn't too late for me. I asked Piff about the best way to cultivate a more compassionate mindset.

"Just get out there," he said. "Get out of your comfort zone. Have more contact with other people. The people who are the most satisfied with their lives are the ones who are the most embedded in their communities and who have engaged in acts of kindness and philanthropy. There's a lot you can get out of being kind to others that money can't buy you."

December 2014

Advanced in years: On the worship of youth

Not long ago, a letter appeared in our local newspaper. In it, the writer argued that the U.S. death toll from COVID-19 (more than 525,000 at this writing) couldn't be compared to the U.S. death tolls of various wars: Korea, 36,574; Vietnam, 58,220; World War II, 405,399; the Civil War, 498,332.

The reason, he wrote, was that wars killed young people. COVID-19, on the other hand, was killing old people.

"The average [age at] death of a soldier," argued the writer, who was in his mid-70s, "is conservatively [estimated at] 25, and if they lived on average to be — again, conservatively — 75, each death represents 50 lost years of life. The most common age of COVID death is over 70, and even with a life expectancy of 85, that's a 15-year loss of life or less.

"A death is a death," he concluded, but averred that even so, a 25-year-old cannot be compared to a 75-year-old.

Many of us feel this way: that the death of a young person is more tragic than the death of an old one. In this calculus, a life's value is determined by the number of years not yet lived, rather than the amount of life experience acquired. This assessment posits that potential life is more valuable than actual life.

If we follow this logic to its end, here's where we find ourselves: believing that the process of living is one of inexorable decline, and that every day we are worth less than we were the day before until, at the end, we find ourselves without any value at all.

David Lancy, an anthropologist and the author of *Raising Children: Surprising Insights from Other Cultures*, coined a term for this kind of mentality, which he found to be prevalent in the United States: He calls it a "neontocracy," meaning it is centered on its children. They are considered the society's most valued members.

Lancy first took note of this in the 1960s, when he was doing fieldwork in Liberia. "In the village I studied, you'd see far more instances of little kids running errands for those who were older, bringing food, bringing tools," he told me. "Children are at their beck and call: 'Go fetch this! Go fetch that!' Any adult in the community, in the village, has the right to tell a kid what to do. It seemed so different from contemporary child rearing in the United States. In our society, we impose very little of our needs on children.

"In our society," he concluded, "children rule."

When Lancy came back to the United States, he started reading ethnographic manuscripts focused on other cultures around the world. After studying more than 1,000 societies, he realized that what he had seen in that Liberian village was the rule and that U.S. culture was the exception. In most places, he found, children are not even considered full persons; instead, personhood is something you earn. "One of the common threads that run through those societies is that children start out with very few expectations, and very little importance," he says.

If our culture can be described as a neontocracy, the arrangement that he found to be more common throughout the world is what he calls a "gerontocracy": a society in which the elders are the most valued members. "In a gerontocracy, your venerable age alone gives you status," Lancy says. "On top of that, good work, hard work, taking care of others — all those things — can enhance your social standing. A child doesn't have any of those experiences. What's considered important is what the child contributes to others and how they contribute to the community as a whole — not what they accomplish on their own. Gerontocracy, in many ways, is much more compatible with our evolution as a species."

How did we in the United States get to be this way? How did we arrive at the point where we worship our children and scorn our elders? According to Lancy, by the middle of the last century, parents began putting their children on a pedestal, and that tendency has increased with every subsequent decade. At the same time, the birthrate was dropping, so in a sense, the value of each child increased. Children also consumed a growing share of family resources.

The American love of youth has deeper roots than that, however. In the late 1800s, historians say, the process of aging came to be seen as a medical problem to be solved. In her book *This Chair Rocks: A Manifesto Against Ageism*, Ashton Applewhite makes the case that this trend accelerated in the 20th century. "Propelled by postwar leisure and prosperity, the explosion of consumer culture, and research into a stage of life newly dubbed 'adolescence,' youth culture emerged as a distinct twentieth-century phenomenon," she writes. "As this 'cult of youth' grew, gerontophobia — fear of aging and dislike, even hatred, of old people — gained traction."

Throughout the 20th century, the status of our elders fell, and today they find themselves at the very bottom of the ladder. We're all future senior citizens, if we're lucky, but we often look down the road with fear and denial. In 2019, Americans spent $53 billion on anti-aging products promising to stave off this natural process, or at least the appearance of it.

Yet among the costs of neontocracy, perhaps the most telling is our underwhelming response to the deaths caused by the pandemic, which has disproportionately killed our elder citizens.

Imagine, for a moment, that COVID-19, when it arrived, killed 80 percent of infected children. There would have been panic. There would have been outrage. And there would have been action and much more serious attempts at controlling the virus, as there were in less youth-centric cultures such as China, Italy, and Spain. We would have taken extreme measures to protect our most valued citizens.

But we didn't. And now the generations that fought in World War II, Korea, and Vietnam are on the front lines of this war, too.

Jim Puppe knows that old age is not a long slide into irrelevance and that getting through life, and through hardship, can increase the value of one's life. Growing up in North Dakota, he heard stories about the Depression, about the "Dirty Thirties" of the Dust Bowl, about World War II, and other challenges that society faced. Yet, he recalls, the people who went through those hard times didn't seem bitter. They didn't seem angry. Rather, they seemed content. In fact, the more adversity they had seen, the more content they were.

Puppe wanted to know why. So in 2004, after he retired, he set out to find one person in each community in his state with wisdom to share. He would show up in a town and ask around for someone with "human spirit, optimism, good morals, values, and integrity" whom he could interview.

More often than not, this was someone older, a person who had made it through tough times. Puppe would sit down with them and listen to what they had to say. At the end of each interview, he would ask what advice the person might have for their grandchildren. "They would say love, respect for others, honesty," he told me when I called him. "But one fellow just sat there for a minute and said, 'I have no advice for them.'

"And I said, 'You don't have any advice for your grandkids?'

"And he said, 'No. Let how I live be my advice.'"

Over 14 years, Puppe visited 617 towns, and he published the stories he collected in a book he titled *Dakota Attitude*. "What they told me was just priceless," he says. "There's a vast resource of knowledge, experience, and wisdom that we can gain from these folks that's been untapped. In my opinion, most of the problems we have in the world today could be solved by a good grandma."

If anything good comes of this pandemic, my hope is that more of us will end up like Jim Puppe, and less like my local letter-writer. I hope we can come to see that life becomes more, not less, valuable with age. And if our culture won't change from its child-centered ways, then let's each create our own small gerontocracy among the people we know — before all that wisdom, all those memories, and all those lives are gone.

May 2021

Less is more: On gluttony and abundance

Not long ago, I found myself at a strange and wondrous place: the All You Can Eat Buffet. There's one in nearly every town in America; no doubt you've been inside. What the food may lack in quality, it makes up for in quantity. As soon as a tray is emptied, a new load of chicken-fried steak, wontons, or pancakes appears.

It's like the children's story *Strega Nona*, in which an unwise Italian villager named Big Anthony turns on a witch's magic pasta pot only to find that he can't turn it off. Soon the town is buried under a mound of spaghetti. When the witch returns, she stops the pot — and makes Big Anthony eat it all. Boy, is he sorry.

At the buffet I kept eating, too, until finally I felt some sympathy for Big Anthony. Yet the pots did have a certain magic; I wondered at the endlessness of the feast. It struck me that we live in an incredible time. As a species, we have been wildly successful, productive beyond our ancestors' dreams. Generations of the past would have hardly believed the quantities available to us today: the mountains of food, the floods of goods, the torrents of information.

In France in the 1700s, people ate an average of 1,600 calories per day; today, the average French diet comes in at around 3,000 calories per day. In 1970, Americans ate 2.3 pounds of food a day; today, we eat about 25 percent more than that.

But we humans didn't achieve all this overnight. Much of this growth took place in the late 20th century, when the global costs of food and fuel plummeted compared with wages, writes food and agricultural policy expert Robert Paarlberg in his 2015 book, *The United States of Excess: Gluttony and the Dark Side of American Exceptionalism*. From 1961 to 2000, for instance, U.S. fruit production grew by 130 percent. (China's, meanwhile, grew by 1,061 percent.)

This apparently favorable circumstance has led to some problems. "Our species has not lost its 'discipline' over food consumption — because we never really had (or needed) that discipline," writes Paarlberg. Our innate drive to consume enough food to survive has become a struggle to keep from eating too much.

That struggle isn't limited to food. We are also buying more things, largely because there are more things to buy and we have more money to buy them with: Between 1870 and 2014, average incomes rose 17 times. (In contrast, from A.D. 1 to 1820, incomes merely doubled.)

Our minds are also coping with a cognitive tsunami: In 2016, all the data on the internet amounted to 1 zettabyte, the equivalent of 152 million years of high-definition video. This year, that will have doubled. As Paarlberg noted about food, so it is with bytes: We humans are not well equipped to deal with this volume of information. In an age without limits, we must figure out strategies to hold back the tide.

We are trying to do that. Today we have the "slow food" movement, which attempts to make dinners more human and healthy by asking us take our time cooking and eating. We have fans of minimalism, which sees people paring down their possessions until their homes look like an Apple Store. We have apps that allow us to shut off the internet so we can give ourselves the space we need to digest the information we have consumed. And we have proponents of intermittent fasting, who abstain from eating one or two days a week as a way to cope with the obscene amounts of food available to modern humans. Interestingly, this approach also seems to offer a range of health benefits.

"What we're finding," says Mark Mattson, a neuroscientist at the National Institute on Aging, "is that when we switch to an intermittent fasting diet, the brain and body change in ways that improve their function and their resistance to stress. These cycles of challenge and recovery seem to optimize health."

For hundreds of thousands of years, of course, fasting wasn't something we chose to do. It was a reflection of life: random and unpredictable. That's the environment we adapted to, and that's the environment we still seem to need. Our bodies and minds were shaped by this ebb and flow. Only now there is no ebb, only flow.

The idea of simplifying one's life is not new, but the current push for it carries a tinge of panic. And while most of us are not going to end up cramming into tiny homes, the idea behind them is worth considering.

"Because food and fuel no longer ration themselves, unprecedented self-disciplines must now be constructed, at both the social and individual level," Paarlberg writes.

Self-discipline is not always a popular idea, but it is an important one. And what people don't realize is that often, it's not about using the force of will to make the right decisions. It's about creating situations in which the decision has already been made.

I think about this every day. It's the reason I've never gotten a smartphone. It's the reason I periodically shut down my social media accounts, and it's the reason I spend part of each day with the internet blocked from my computer.

I don't dislike having so much information at my fingertips. And I like keeping up with what my friends are doing, thinking, and eating. If anything, I like it too much. Trying to take it all in leaves me feeling fragmented, disordered, and rudderless. I need a quiet space, and after a certain amount of solitude, I always feel I am better able to navigate my world.

As a parent of 10- and 12-year-old daughters, I have to think about these things for them as well. One popular approach among parents these days is to have their child sign a "contract" to get a phone. These often spell out rules and expectations: *I will not take inappropriate photos. I will not bully. I will tell you if I am bullied. I will not use my phone at the table. I will not believe everything I read, hear, or see online. I will not give out my private information. I will be kind.*

Such contracts read like wish lists for the kind of person parents hope their child will be — and for the kind of world they want their child to live in. But as I think about the world I want for my daughters, I find there's something missing from those pledges — something that seems like the most important thing of all: *I promise to keep a quiet space for myself. I promise to step away when the flow becomes too much. I promise to find some quiet hilltop in my life where I can go to think about who I am and who I want to be.*

We have worked to banish hunger from our bodies and minds, only to find that we need some challenge, some scarcity, and some empty space to survive after all. Now that we've turned on all these magic pots, like Big Anthony, we've got to conjure a way to stop them.

March 2019

Too much information: On gluttony and unplugging

About a year ago, I made a radical pledge. It came after several years of feeling less and less able to deal with the tidal wave of information coming at me: 3.6 zettabytes annually, which amounts to 100,000 words each day. That's a 350 percent increase over people's exposure in 1980.

I was drowning in data. So, like an electronic-age Dutch boy, I put my finger in the dike. Each Monday, I resolved, I would spend the entire day offline.

I didn't make this decision lightly. As a writer, I depend on the internet to find information, to communicate with friends and colleagues, and to refill the well of knowledge and ideas. Yet the costs of constant access were becoming impossible to ignore. Sometimes I would go online to find one thing, then spend an hour or two reading about other interesting things, while completely forgetting what I had originally been looking for. I couldn't focus. I couldn't keep my thoughts straight. Sometimes I felt like I was losing my mind.

I was — I am — sane. But my brain — as *Future Shock* author Alvin Toffler wrote, and *The Rotarian* excerpted in July 1970 — was being forced to process information at a much higher volume than it is equipped to handle. "What consequences this [cognitive overstimulation] may have for mental health in the techno-societies," Toffler wrote ominously, "has yet to be determined."

Living in the future that Toffler envisioned, I was starting to get a read on those consequences: the gnawing unease, the accelerating slide down a scree slope of trivia, the feeling that my mind was a balloon with a million tiny holes. Every time I turned on my computer, it was akin to opening a floodgate, when all I wanted was to sit and focus, taking in information clearly and steadily, like a drink from a cool mountain stream.

I now know I am not alone. We are finding out that our brains did not evolve to be bombarded with ceaseless novelty and stimuli. Multitasking is not the wave of the future. Forty years after Toffler raised the issue, scientists are starting to uncover the fallout.

They are learning, for example, that those who attempt to perform two different tasks simultaneously end up doing neither task well, and that multitasking "prevents people from getting a deeper understanding of information," in the words of one researcher. One study shows a 10-point drop in IQ scores after constant distractions from email, text messaging, and cell phones.

Some evidence also suggests that the perpetual navigation and endless choices that come with being online contribute to something called "ego depletion," or the running down of our willpower. That would explain why I often emerged lethargic, unsatisfied, and oddly exhausted after a day of sitting alone at my desk, trying to decide which way to steer my digital rudder.

At the same time, researchers are finding that idleness, even daydreaming, is essential for the brain to process new information and integrate it into long-term memory, storing it where we can actually use it.

The first Monday of my new life came around. I turned on my out-of-office response for my email. I set a program I'd found called SelfControl, which lets you lock yourself out of specific websites and email servers, to eight hours. I took a breath. I hit start.

There is a scene in *2001: A Space Odyssey* in which one of the astronauts is flying into the void of space, trying to reinsert his air tube. That's how it felt to me. Strange. Cold. Alone. Quiet. It was like finding myself on the moon, staring back at earth. I knew there was a lot going on down there. I knew there was a great party I was missing. I longed to rejoin the digital throng. I knew there was some deathly important email that needed addressing. I was sure someone would call, wondering why I hadn't responded.

No one did. I sat down and finished a few small projects I'd been putting off. I thought through my week and made a list of things that needed to be done. I wrote emails to send later. I jotted down things to look up. I organized some research. I enjoyed the sense of having some space in my head where there was room for new ideas.

I even had time to sit down and read a book.

By the end of the day, I felt something that I hadn't in a long time: a sense of accomplishment. And when I finally logged on to see what I had missed, I was surprised by the answer: not much.

I began the next day refreshed. I whipped through my emails and got on with things, a little more in control. The rest of the week had a linear coherence I hadn't even realized I'd missed. I was starting to get my mind back. The next week, my day offline was easier, and the week after that easier still. I tried not to be dogmatic about it. Sometimes I would check my email midday. Sometimes I would be offline Tuesday instead of Monday. But the principle was the same: at least one full day unplugged.

As time went on, I noticed my anxiety level going down, my energy coming up, my focus returning, and the false sense of urgency that the internet seems to foster disappearing. If the internet does change your brain, the good news is that you can still change it back.

Now I spend part of every day — and sometimes several days at a time — offline. SelfControl the program has been gradually supplemented by self-control the actual skill. I have started to understand that I can function efficiently in the information age after all. And when I see the tidal wave coming at me, instead of letting it wash over me, swamping my little boat, I think I've found a way to keep my hand on the tiller and enjoy the ride.

April 2011

Invisible links: On the smallness of the world

If I close my eyes, I can almost remember how far away Wuhan, China, felt a year ago. When the news broke that something terrible was happening there, I couldn't picture the place. Nor did I think it would have anything to do with me. I had no idea that what was transpiring there could affect — or infect — my life in Minnesota.

But soon enough I knew all about Wuhan. I knew that some people who had visited a seafood market there had gotten sick, and that that sickness had spiraled through the city, then through the world. I remember marveling at how this tiny organism — just a strand of DNA — could leap from one person to another, to another, crossing the planet like a frog hopping across a pond, before arriving at my door.

In January 2020, our family had been on vacation in Mexico City. Not long after we returned, one of my daughters came down with a fever so high we were minutes away from taking her to the hospital. The fever went down, only to be followed by a racking cough that lasted for weeks. A few days later, my wife and I had the same cough, which lasted months. We still have no idea if this was COVID-19, but either way, it was a reminder of the invisible threads that reach around the world, connecting us all.

Before the pandemic, I felt isolated from places so far away. But as Anthony Fauci noted back in 2017 — before the immunologist became a household name — that feeling was misguided. "The mistake that so many people have made," Fauci said in a talk at Georgetown University Medical Center, "is a failure to look beyond our own borders in the issue of the globality of health issues."

That was a mistake I made not just about health issues, but about all issues. Even though I came of age in the era of globalization, of international travel, of effortless border crossings, I failed to fully comprehend that with 7.8 billion people alive today, the world is smaller than it has ever been.

This notion isn't new. It was in 1929, when there were only about 2 billion people in the world, that the person credited with popularizing the idea, a Hungarian writer named Frigyes Karinthy, published a short story called "Chain-Links."

"Let me put it this way," the main character in the story says. "Planet Earth has never been as tiny as it is now. It shrunk — relatively speaking, of course — due to the quickening pulse of both physical and verbal communication." Another character makes a bet that "using no more than five individuals, one of whom is a personal acquaintance," he could contact anyone in the world.

From Karinthy's story emerged the concept of "six degrees of separation," the belief that we are connected to every other person on earth by no more than five other people.

On the surface, this is counterintuitive. If there are more people in the world than ever, shouldn't two random people be further removed from each other? No: because the more people there are, the more connections in the network, and the more ways for information — and viruses — to travel.

This paradox, termed the "small world problem," was tested by the legendary psychologist Stanley Milgram in the 1960s. Milgram gave volunteers in Nebraska and in Boston instructions to forward a packet to a specific businessman in Boston using only acquaintances. And while many of the packets didn't arrive, those that did made it via a chain of, on average, 5.2 connections.

Milgram's experiment had some flaws, but the idea that we are only five people away from any other person on the planet became lodged in the collective mind. In 1994, three college students in Pennsylvania invented a game called Six Degrees of Kevin Bacon, in which, jumping from film to film, players link any actor to a movie featuring Bacon. Mathematicians now play Six Degrees of Paul Erdos, in which they see how closely linked, via co-authors, their papers are to those of Erdos, a Hungarian mathematician who published more than 1,500 papers. The idea of those six degrees has inspired plays, TV shows, and films. An early social media site was called sixdegrees.com (apparently, a degree too far to catch on).

The idea has also inspired additional research, some of which confirms this "small world" effect. In 2007, researchers at Microsoft and Carnegie Mellon looked at 30 billion Microsoft Messenger conversations and found that "the average path length among Messenger users is 6.6" people. In 2011, researchers found "an average degree of separation of 3.43 between two random Twitter users."

Researchers at Facebook found that the number of intermediaries went down as the number of people in the pool grew. In 2011, they estimated that an average of 3.74 people connected random Facebook users. By 2016, the number of people on Facebook had doubled to 1.6 billion and that figure had dropped to 3.57.

We are often surprised when we encounter this phenomenon in real life. Some years ago, my wife and I were staying in a hostel in New Zealand. There we met a young German woman who mentioned that she had been an exchange student in the United States. We asked her where, and she replied that it was a small town in the Midwest that we had probably never heard of. But we had heard of it: She had attended the very school where my mother-in-law worked as a counselor.

Experiences like that can make your head spin, though they shouldn't. As the pandemic has shown us, our connections, even when invisible, are real. And these chain-links affect us in ways we rarely appreciate.

We are a social species. Humans evolved in small groups that needed to work together to survive. Today, our groups are bigger, but we're no less social. The evolutionary psychologist and anthropologist Robin Dunbar has formulated the "social brain" theory, which maintains that the evolutionary increases in the size of our brains were driven by our need to socially navigate the groups of people around us.

To successfully live and work with others, we have to understand them. This is a complex process that compels us to continually try to read each other's minds. The flow of information between people is constant, and we use it to glean the intentions of those around us. Our brain is both a radar for human-related information and a learning machine. Much of what it learns comes from other people.

Our need to be close to others means that we catch ideas from each other. We also catch ailments that are not obviously contagious. Soon after the reunification of Germany in 1990, a national health survey found that East and West Germany had starkly different rates of lower back pain. The disparity was as high as 16 percent. In a paper titled "Back Pain, a Communicable Disease?" the authors showed how, after 45 years of separation came to an end, levels of lower back pain in the former East Germany slowly rose until they finally reached West German levels in 1996. After that, the rates moved in unison.

This kind of contagion may be surprising, but it is ubiquitous. In a study published in 2008, James Fowler and Nicholas Christakis looked at data from the Framingham Heart Study (a study of cardiovascular disease that has been ongoing since 1948) and found they could map the way happiness spreads through our connections with friends and acquaintances. A friend who lives within a mile of you and who becomes happy increases your likelihood of being happy by 25 percent, and vice versa. This flow continues, at lower levels, through two more degrees of separation, and it can be observed in many other areas of life as well: creativity, joy, depression, obesity, financial panic, smoking, and quitting smoking.

Fowler and Christakis wrote a book about this, titled *Connected: The Surprising Power of Our Social Networks and How They Shape Our Lives.* "Everything we do or say tends to ripple through our network, having an impact on our friends (one degree), our friends' friends (two degrees), and even our friends' friends' friends (three degrees)," they wrote.

The authors call this the "Three Degrees of Influence" rule. "If we are connected to everyone else by six degrees, and we can influence them up to three degrees, then one way to think about ourselves is that each of us can reach about halfway to everyone else on the planet," they wrote.

There are many contagious things in this world, and many paths by which those things can travel. As humans, we are nurtured by things like friendship, kindness, and goodwill that come to us along those pathways. But the tiny organism that is COVID-19 is taking advantage of our need for connection, for proximity, for being part of a group. It is turning something that was our greatest strength into its own.

"Everything returns and renews itself," Karinthy wrote in 1929. "The difference now is that the rate of these returns has increased, in both space and time, in an unheard-of fashion. Now my thoughts can circle the globe in minutes. Entire passages of world history are played out in a couple of years."

It feels like many years since I first heard of Wuhan, though it's been only one. For me, the pandemic has been a wake-up call. It has made me realize that while there may be 7.8 billion people on earth, and we may speak thousands of languages, you can't simply shut your door to keep it all out. Distance is an illusion. Wuhan is right next door. We can't always choose what comes our way, but we can choose what we send out, rippling across the world.

Like it or not, we're all in this together.

March 2021

That's what friends are for: On loneliness and connection

Some years ago, before my wife and I had kids, we moved to a town in Wisconsin where we had no real ties. We made a few friends, but none of them had ties there either, and within a few years they'd nearly all moved away.

After our first daughter was born, we became consumed with the duties of modern parenthood. Still, we tried to find our community. Sometimes on a walk, I would try to think of someone I could drop in on to say hello, but there was no one. I tried to imagine who might notice if we picked up and left town, but hardly anyone came to mind.

A common measure of social connection is the number of people you can call on in an emergency. In that town, I couldn't think of a soul.

Then I started having a strange fear. Whenever we were away for any period of time, I became sure that our house had burned down. My wife found this alarming and paranoid.

It was. In retrospect, I know it was a sign of something deeply wrong. It was becoming hard for me to envision a future in which my life was intertwined with the lives of others. The fear of fire, I think, pointed to the fact that everything that mattered to me was contained within the walls of our home.

In psychology, there's a school of thought that holds that our identity, our "self," is a story we tell ourselves. We recall the important events in our lives and the way they have made us into who we are. The flip side, however, is that everyone's story needs an audience, real or imagined. The longer we lived in that town, the harder I found it to imagine any such audience. To me, that is the essence of loneliness.

At my wife's behest, we sold our house and headed north to a city in Minnesota, one where we had family and friends. Slowly, the balance between solitude and social life tipped back.

That period of my life left some scars that took a while to heal. But it also led me to ask myself some questions that until then I'd never had to confront. I'd never had a problem making friends. It had never occurred to me that this could be a problem. I'd always had friends and assumed I always would. Now I knew that wasn't necessarily so.

Around the turn of the last century, a young man who'd moved to Chicago from a smaller town had the same realization. "There is no place like a city park on a Sunday afternoon to feel one's loneliness," wrote Paul Harris in his memoir *My Road to Rotary*. "To me one essential was lacking, the presence of friends. Emerson said, 'He who has a thousand friends has not a friend to spare.' In my earliest days in my adopted city, I had neither the thousand nor the one."

In 1905, Harris addressed this problem by organizing the first Rotary club. "I was sure that there must be many other young men who had come from farms and small villages to establish themselves in Chicago," he wrote. "In fact I knew a few. Why not bring them together? If the others were longing for fellowship as I was, something would come of it."

Something did. By the time Harris died in 1947, Rotary International had nearly 300,000 members, many of whom were seeking fellowship. Today that number is 1.2 million. Yet only recently have we started to understand exactly how important a role an organization like this can play in our lives.

"Loneliness is an enormous health problem," says Lydia Denworth, author of *Friendship: The Evolution, Biology, and Extraordinary Power of Life's Fundamental Bond*. "It's a really serious problem that we used to think was this minor emotion. We understand now how bad it is for you."

Loneliness increases your risk of heart attack, stroke, and dementia. It impairs your immune system. It puts you at higher risk for depression, anxiety, and suicide. Lonely people, one study found, are 26 percent more likely to die prematurely than those who are not lonely — a risk on par with smoking and obesity.

While it's been widely reported that there's an epidemic of loneliness in America today, Denworth disputes this. According to some studies, loneliness has increased slightly, but not significantly.

People's core relationships remain more stable than those news reports would lead us to believe; it's more the case that most of us feel lonely at some point in our lives.

Friendship, which Denworth defines as "a close bond that's long-lasting, positive, and cooperative," is a core biological necessity. It's part of what the researcher and social psychologist Roy Baumeister and his colleagues termed "the need to belong," an evolutionary drive that underlies almost every aspect of our psychology.

"Friendship isn't a cultural extra," says Denworth. "It's feeding a fundamental drive to connect and a need to belong." The science of friendship, she says, gives us "permission to hang out with our friends, and recognize that we're doing something good for us."

In her book *Love 2.0: Finding Happiness and Health in Moments of Connection*, Barbara L. Fredrickson, the director of the Positive Emotions and Psychophysiology Laboratory at the University of North Carolina at Chapel Hill, writes that three things happen when you connect with another person: a sharing of positive emotions, a synchronizing of brain activity known as "neural coupling," and a reflected interest in each other's well-being. This can happen with any person you know, and Fredrickson argues that this connection is actually what we mean when we talk about "love."

She also notes something Paul Harris would have appreciated: True connection wants physical proximity. We best connect with someone, in a biologically satisfying way, if we're in the same room.

Friendship may be deeply biological, but it's also cultural, and people around the world define it differently. In the Papua New Guinea Highlands, writes anthropologist Daniel Hruschka in his cross-cultural study *Friendship: Development, Ecology and Evolution of a Relationship*, friends among the Wandeki people greet each other by shouting, "I should like to eat your intestines!" and responding, "Yes, I too should like to eat your intestines." In north-central Africa, Zande "blood brothers" consume each other's blood to ensure the friendship will last. In Japan, there are different words for different kinds of friends. For example, young children have playmates (*tomodachi*) while older children have close friends (*shinyuu*). And among the Tausug people in the Philippines, a "blood friend" can be counted on to "assist with debts, to loan guns if needed, to provide food and shelter, and to come to his aid in a fight," Hruschka writes.

Americans value things like "self-disclosure" (sharing secrets) and informality in our friendships. But not everyone feels the same way. Of the 400 cultures Hruschka analyzed, only 33 percent prized self-disclosure and 28 percent valued informality. Much more common across all cultures were mutual aid (93 percent), "positive affect," or warmth, affection, and closeness (78 percent), and gift-giving (60 percent).

Despite those differences, every culture has some form of friendship, or "friend-like relationship," as Hruschka calls it. But no matter what we call it, and no matter how much ideas of friendship differ across the world, there's something at its core that we all need.

Julie Beck, an editor at *The Atlantic*, became fascinated with the varieties of the friendship experience, which she writes about in a series called "The Friendship Files."

"What's really interesting to me about friendship is that it doesn't have a set cultural script in the way other relationships have," Beck says. "You meet someone. You like each other. Then everything after that is up to the friends themselves."

Beck has interviewed people who met on Bumble BFF, an app for finding friends. She's talked to a group of friends who've been playing the same game of Dungeons & Dragons for 30 years. She wrote about two friends who live a mile and half apart and walk to the midpoint between their homes each week to give each other a high five.

"One recurring theme," Beck says, "is that it helps to have a structure or a container for your friendship; some kind of built-in ritual that helps you stay in contact. It's not imperative, and it doesn't much matter what it is, but it helps you avoid slipping into that zone where you keep meaning to reach out, but you're busy or you forget."

Ritual or no, making and maintaining friendships takes time. According to research cited by Denworth, it takes 40 to 60 hours to move from being an acquaintance to a casual friend, 80 to 100 hours to become a friend, and 200 hours to earn consideration as a best friend. That adds up to 40 Rotary meetings just to reach the most basic rung of friendship.

"I don't think we understand just how much time it takes to get close to people," she says. "Work and family are important, but so are your friends. We should strive to give it more time, even at busy times of our lives. We think of friendship as a want, but it's a need. It's not a luxury. It's part of our infrastructure."

August 2021

BELIEF

Decline to decline: On aging and expectations

When I turned 40, my younger brother gave me a joke gift: adult diapers. A few years later, when he turned 40, I gave them back. Touché!

The message behind this joke was not subtle: You're old, and your body is going to stop working. In fact, for practically every birthday after the 18th, there are hundreds of cards with the same corny jokes about your failing memory and your sagging body. They're so ubiquitous they seem harmless.

At the time, I thought it was all in good fun. But lately I've been wondering if that is the case. Recently, I listened to a successful national radio commentator — a man in his 60s — bending over backward to avoid saying how old he was. I was struck by the strangeness of it. Why would he be ashamed of having lived so much life? Why did he want so desperately to seem younger than he was?

As I inch closer to 50 myself, I don't feel particularly decrepit. I still travel, and I have plenty of energy and lots of things I want to do. A few years ago I even started running ultramarathons. Yet every time I have a birthday or shop for a birthday card, I'm struck by the mix of ridicule and despair with which we mark each passing year. It gets harder and harder to find a birthday card that is celebratory.

America has always been a country that celebrated youth. But according to one study, it was around 1880 that attitudes toward older people started to become significantly more negative. It was due partly to the increasing "medicalization" of old age, as well as the growing portion of the population over 65. And according to Robert Pogue Harrison, author of *Juvenescence: A Cultural History of Our Age*, our youth worship has only increased since the end of World War II.

Recently I picked up a copy of *There Are No Grownups: A Midlife Coming-of-Age Story* by Paris-based journalist Pamela Druckerman. Ostensibly, it's a book about what it's like to be in your 40s. The book has some funny and insightful essays about that — but mixed in is a steady stream of jokes about declining looks, declining memory, and declining relevance, which contributed to my declining enjoyment.

This is not because I'm afraid of getting old. I am not. But in the past, our love of youth was tempered by a respect for age. Now we think of aging as simply an inexorable decline that ends in death. And our fear of death has become pathological.

Emblematic of this is biomedical gerontologist and mathematician Aubrey de Grey, who assures us that soon people will live to be 1,000, if not forever. De Grey first put forward his ideas for eliminating aging in his 1999 book, *The Mitochondrial Free Radical Theory of Aging*, published when he was 36. He went on to found the SENS Research Foundation, with the goal of curing aging. De Grey is now 55, and we are no closer to that goal.

More acute than our fear of death, however, is our fear of decline — which can be a self-fulfilling prophecy. In a landmark 1979 "counterclockwise" study, Harvard psychologist Ellen Langer took a group of eight elderly men, measured their biomarkers of aging, then took them on a retreat to a location she had decorated to look and feel like 1959.

After living for a week in a world that looked and felt 20 years younger, Langer measured the participants' biomarkers again. The men were found to have improved hearing, better memory, more grip strength, and increased joint flexibility and dexterity. They were taller and their fingers were longer. More than half of them were smarter. In photos taken after the study, the participants were judged, by impartial observers, to be younger than in photos taken beforehand.

Much of what we fear about aging — such as losing our hearing, eyesight, mobility, or memories — may actually be caused in part by our belief that we will lose those things. One study led by Yale School of Public Health psychologist Becca Levy found that people who hold a negative view of aging die an average of 7.5 years before those with a positive view of it. Another study found that women who believed they were at risk from heart disease were 3.6 times more likely to die of heart attacks than women with the same risk factors who believed they weren't.

Levy has spent years investigating this question. It's something that she started thinking about when she was on a fellowship in Japan. "I was really interested in how differently the culture acted toward older members of society, and the different views of aging that were expressed," she says now. "At the time, Japan had the longest life span, and I thought that was really interesting."

She wondered: Was there some relationship between these things? Or did the fact that people lived longer cause them to be more respected? Or was it simply random?

Levy has found that our personal perceptions about getting older have a major impact on how we age. "These views of aging do seem to have an impact on cognitive and physical health," she says. "And in cultures that promote more positive views of aging, individuals who have taken in more of those beliefs have a health advantage over time."

Negative stereotypes start at a very early age — as young as three years old — but don't become harmful until they are "self-relevant." At that point, they can cause us to lose mobility, balance, strength, eyesight, hearing, and memory, and can increase our odds of dementia, Alzheimer's, and cardiovascular events. They may even accelerate our cellular decay.

The good news is that positive aging stereotypes can have the opposite effect. In a study that echoed Langer's "counter-clockwise" findings, Levy found that by subliminally giving older people positive aging stereotypes, after just four weeks, subjects showed improved strength, gait, and balance. Positive beliefs about aging can have a wide range of health benefits in addition to increased mobility: better hearing, memory, and cognitive function. Levy and her colleagues found that veterans who held positive aging stereotypes had significantly lower rates of suicidal thoughts, anxiety, and PTSD. She also found that among carriers of the APOE ε4 gene — one of the strongest predictors of dementia — people with positive age stereotypes were 50 percent less likely to develop the condition.

This does not, of course, mean that you can believe your way to eternal youth. But it does mean that a significant part of our old-age decline may be the direct result of our — and our culture's — belief in it. According to Levy, the first step toward changing this "is to notice it, mark it, realize when it's happening, and question it."

Another step is to realize that the human body is not a car and that "curing" aging is not a matter of replacing parts. A car's decline is a straight line down from the assembly line. A human body grows, evolves, matures, and changes over time, as does the person within it.

But even more important, I think, is that we need to question our assumption that youth is the best time in life and that everything after it is worse. We all know there are good and bad things about every stage in life. Getting older can mean getting better at what you do, being less foolish and self-absorbed than your younger self, and enjoying a richer perspective, more experience, and a store of good memories.

Constantly looking to the past is not only bad for your health, but it makes it harder to find the joy in the present. We can choose to see ourselves as rotting or as ripening with age. Ultimately, we know that life begins and life ends. It's the finite amount in between that makes it sweet.

December 2018

Hope is not enough: On hardship and resilience

A few years ago, I was passing through the northern Nigerian city of Kano when I stopped at a roadside stall for some tea. The proprietor asked me where I was from. I told him.

"I want to go to America!" he told me, smiling. "We are just suffering here in Nigeria. If I go to America, I will not come back to Nigeria again."

"Not even to see your mother?" I asked.

He laughed. "I will send her some money."

I thanked him and drank my tea. After I left, I wondered if he was serious or just talking.

As I traveled through the region, I met several people headed north, on their way to Europe. It was a difficult and dangerous journey that tens of thousands of people set out on each year, many of them never reaching their destination. I often marveled at the confidence a person must have to embark on a trip like that, to leave everything behind, to be certain of somehow making it.

Like most people, I'd always assumed these travelers were the most poverty-stricken, the most hopeless. But now I can see that this isn't the case — at least not entirely. Often, the people who leave their villages are the brightest and most ambitious ones, the ones with the biggest dreams. As one poet from Cameroon wrote after arriving in Spain, "No money in the pockets/But hope in the heart." Hope, as much as anything else, drives them.

Hope may be our most important asset as a species. Hope is the thing that drew us out of our caves and around the world. Hope is what gets us out of bed in the morning. Hope lets us imagine our lives as more than they are. Yet when we talk about hope, we usually mean the vague feeling that things will get better. But that is not hope.

One of the foremost experts on the science of hope, the late C.R. Snyder, defined it as "a learned way of thinking about oneself in relation to goals" and noted that it is "the essential process of linking oneself to potential success." Hope is having confidence that you can do what you set out to do, whether that is crossing a desert or getting a job or mastering a craft. "High-hope" individuals, as a result, have more goals overall, more difficult goals, and more success at achieving those goals than "low-hope" people. They are also happier, recover more quickly from physical injuries, and have less work-related burnout. Most important, they see themselves as being in control of their lives.

Snyder believed this is a quality that can be cultivated, and one that develops early in life. Hope is born from struggle — from learning that we can rise to the challenges life presents. And we, in turn, are born to deal with struggle. In his 1994 book *The Psychology of Hope*, Snyder cited studies that found that if you give toddlers a choice of two toys, one freely available and the other behind a barrier, they will almost invariably be drawn to the one behind the barrier. And when they achieve a goal, such as figuring out how to get that toy, they become more confident that they will achieve others. This has a protective effect for the challenges that lie ahead. This is how we learn to hope.

When I read this, I thought back to Nigeria, and to other parts of Africa, where there is no shortage of daily struggle. Was that why so many people kept getting into rickety boats to cross the Mediterranean? Was that why my ancestors came from Europe to America, full of hope? Was it because of the hard lives they'd had — the challenges they had already overcome?

If so, this raises some questions for those of us in wealthy countries, where it sometimes seems that our main pursuit is a life devoid of discomforts. Today, the trend among parents is to smooth the road in front of our children. We put rubber bumpers on every surface. We cook special meals. We help write college entrance essays. We don't want our children to fall, to fail, or to be hurt in any way. We want them to have an easy life.

As the father of two girls, I've tried to avoid this, but it doesn't always go over well. One day we were at a playground, and I was reading a magazine when I heard someone yelling: "Sir! Sir!" I looked up to see who was being called, and saw a man pointing at me and gesticulating wildly. "Sir!" he said. "Your daughter is going to fall!"

I jumped up. There was my youngest (then around three), standing on a platform about as tall as my head. She was holding on to a bar and leaning out over the sandy ground. I could see she was trying to figure out a way down, but kids kept coming up the way she wanted to go. I stood there for a minute, trapped between humiliation and relief. Then I sat back down and watched her finally make her way down by another route.

I worry sometimes about this collective effort to make our children's lives easier. And I'm not the only one. The writer Luke Epplin notes that children's films have been taken over by what he calls the "magic feather syndrome," in which a character's greatest liability suddenly helps him magically realize his impossible dreams. "It's enough," he writes, "for [the protagonists] simply to show up with no experience at the world's most competitive races, dig deep within themselves, and out-believe their opponents." Their only struggle, in other words, is not having what they want. They overcome this by wanting harder.

I don't want my daughters to feel that is what they should expect. So when my older daughter turned six and we gave her a choice of any movie to watch, I was relieved and heartened when she picked a film made long before convenience and comfort became human rights. I was glad to hear her say she wanted to watch *Old Yeller*.

The movie had come up in a discussion about rabies. I knew it was a hard one, and I made sure she knew what she was in for. Even when I told her the end, she held firm, so we all sat down to watch it. There was more to it than I remembered. It starts with 14-year-old Travis being left with his mother and brother while his father goes on a months-long cattle drive. Travis has to deal with razorback boars, lecherous neighbors, attacking bears, and the rabid wolf Yeller fights off.

There are no magic feathers. It's a surprisingly honest film, with none of today's happily-ever-after platitudes. It felt real in a way kids' movies don't anymore. At the end, Travis' father comes home and pulls him aside.

"Now and then," he tells Travis, "for no good reason a man can figure out, life will just haul off and knock him flat. But it's not all like that. ... And you can't afford to waste the good part fretting about the bad."

That was what I wanted my daughter to hear, and to know. Life is hard. You fall, then you get back up. Then you keep going. Hope is not magic. Hope is hard-won. Hope is not what you have. Hope is what you do.

January 2015

Beyond belief: On self-deception

One evening, sitting in the back seat of the car, our two girls, ages six and eight, were discussing the show we were on our way to attend. Called The Illusionists, it featured seven of the world's top magicians. The debate consisted of whether there would be real magic involved, or just tricks.

"When they cut the man in half," our younger daughter asked, "how do they keep the blood in?" She was convinced there was true magic. Her older sister, a little wiser, wasn't buying it.

"Easy," she said. "R-o-b-o-t." She rolled her eyes at how obvious this was. During the show, sure enough, we came to the part where a man — standing up, no less — was sawed in half. His torso fell onto a table, while his legs walked offstage. His top half was wheeled around before us, perfectly animate, perfectly alive.

It was clearly not a robot. Yet what it was, none of us could imagine. And even if we could have found out how it worked, I'd almost rather not. Because in a sense, both girls were right: There was real magic and there were tricks. The magic is in wondering how you were tricked. That's why we go to see performances like the Illusionists.

Humans are not hard to deceive. If we were, most political careers would be much shorter. Our gullibility has even played an important role in our own evolution. In his book, *Sapiens: A Brief History of Humankind*, historian Yuval Noah Harari argues that the agricultural revolution was a trick played on humans — by plants. Wheat, rice, and potatoes, with all their delicious flavors, enticed us to spread their DNA around the planet by trading our hunter-gatherer lifestyle for a much tougher farming one. Wheat went from being a wild grass in Turkey to covering an area of the earth 10 times the size of Great Britain. We like to tell ourselves that we conquered nature with agriculture. But, Harari says, the opposite is true: "These plants domesticated Homo sapiens, rather than vice versa."

Deception may not always be a bad thing: There's some evidence, for example, that depression is the result not of a distorted view of reality but of an all-too-clear one, known as "depressive realism." Do hope and optimism actually require a certain amount of self-deception? Psychologist Joanna Starek found that athletes who scored higher on measures of self-deception also performed better, suggesting that sometimes you may have to trick yourself into believing you can do something before you can do it. And if what you're trying to do has never been done before, you must first deceive yourself into believing it can be done.

There is, of course, a dark side to self-deception: Our beliefs and biases blind us to things we need to see. As the philosopher Friedrich Nietzsche once observed, "Convictions are more dangerous enemies of truth than lies."

Political scientists Brendan Nyhan and Jason Reifler conducted a series of experiments that show how true this is. We all have biases and ideologies, and those can lead us to become badly misinformed, even about basic facts. In various studies, Nyhan and Reifler gave people empirically correct information in the form of a news article meant to correct a misperception — that Barack Obama is Muslim, that Mitt Romney shipped jobs overseas, that cutting taxes increases revenue to the treasury, that the measles-mumps-rubella vaccine causes autism. All these statements are false, so correcting them should be a simple matter of presenting people with the correct information. But as with the Illusionists, things are not quite as they seem. What Nyhan and Reifler found was that presenting the correct information often had the opposite effect: It caused people to believe the wrong information even more strongly.

They call this the "backfire effect," and the reasons behind it are complicated. One is the echo chambers people create for themselves in the friends they associate with and the media they follow. Another has to do with "motivated reasoning."

"In any given situation," Nyhan says, "you have some level of motivation to determine the correct answer. That's called accuracy motivation. And you also have some motivation to find the answer that you'd like to be true."

We each have an ideology — an idea about how the world works — and we want information to fit into that scheme. When we're presented with facts that don't fit, or worse, that contradict our beliefs, we often choose to dismiss them rather than to reconsider our assumptions.

After all, who has the time and energy to come up with a new ideology every time we're wrong about something? There is a particular kind of panic that sets in when our belief system begins to crumble. It's easy to have a clear system that tells you what is right and what is wrong. It is much harder to ask, at every juncture, whether you could be wrong.

More recently, Nyhan and Reifler have begun researching ways to counter the backfire effect. One strategy that seems to work is to present correct information in graphic form, rather than as text. Another is what they call "affirmation" — having subjects write an essay about a value that has been important to them, or a time when they felt really good about themselves.

The latter approach increases the rate of correction among some (though not all) subjects. The underlying idea is that by reaffirming our values and self-worth, we don't feel the same level of "identity threat" from information that runs counter to our beliefs. Being aware of our values can make us more open to new information that goes against those beliefs.

There is no easy answer to this dilemma, no magic formula for how much clarity and how much cloudiness we should expect in life. But none of us will ever see the world with perfect accuracy all the time — nor would we want to. In a sense, each of us is the illusionist in our own show. The secret is to know when to be brave and pull back the veil on our own tricks, and when to leave it drawn and simply wonder at the magic.

April 2015

The good-enough life: On Gandhi and a girl

The first class I took in college was a history of India structured around the life of Gandhi. I wasn't all that interested in India, but I was concerned about my role in the world. I wanted to be a good person — or at least a better one. I wanted to leave the world a better place. I wanted to do no harm. I wanted to live a good life, an ethical life, one that I could be proud of when it was all over.

But what is the right thing to do? Ever since Aristotle, people have been trying to create ethical systems that would tell you. John Stuart Mill thought the right thing was whatever contributed to the greatest happiness of the greatest number of people. More recently, ethical thinkers have parsed evolutionary research for understanding and instruction.

Gandhi, I thought at the time, must have something to offer along these lines. After all, using a nonviolent approach, he defeated British colonialism. He developed a philosophy that revolved around *satyagraha*, or soul force, and *ahimsa*, or doing no harm. Things, for him, seemed clear: He knew what was right and wrong and what to fight for and how to do it. He lived according to his principles. I wanted to live like that too. Gandhi was known as "Mahatma," or the Great Soul. I wanted my soul to be great too.

On our first day of class, a pretty girl with brown eyes and auburn hair sat next to me. She wrote her name on the seating chart: Bridgit. She had grown up in a town not far from mine, and we knew some of the same people. Within a few weeks, we were dating. We never ran out of things to talk about. We laughed a lot. She was studying to be a social worker and was also concerned about leaving the world a little better off.

As the class went on, I fell deeper in love, both with her and with Gandhi. I got involved with Amnesty International and would stay up late, neglecting my homework, because there were still more letters to write on behalf of political prisoners around the world. I joined an environmental group and dreamed of going off the grid, of radical simplicity, of zero impact. Instead of a drinking glass, I used an old pop can, because it was still perfectly good. I couldn't come up with any justification for throwing it away. I had no idea where to draw the lines. I gradually grew more ascetic.

Bridgit, however, had a more nuanced idea of what it meant to be a good person, or to live a good life. She was reading the same books on Gandhi and respected what he'd done — she even believed in a certain amount of *ahimsa*. But she also could see how, while he preached kindness, he was an autocratic husband and father. For her, a good life meant striking a balance between the causes you believed in and the people you loved, between the world and your home, between your ideals and your community.

One day, I was sitting in my darkened dorm room, bundled in my fair-trade Guatemalan sweater, reading a Noam Chomsky book and tinkering with a solar panel I'd recently bought, when Bridgit came over to discuss the direction things were going. I remember her words: "I'm not going to marry Gandhi."

At the time, I wasn't thinking of getting married. But the words penetrated my moralistic fog. I was being offered a choice: a life with her, or a life alone with my principles. It was, perhaps, my first glimpse of the notion that selflessness can be a kind of selfishness, that morality can be a kind of narcissism. Maybe choosing to be a good person wasn't as simple as Gandhi had made it seem. But how do you balance what you owe the world with what you owe the people around you?

It's a question most of us ask at some point in our lives. There is never a clear answer. In a way, it is a version of the classic ethical dilemma: Is it better to steal food to feed your family, or to let your family starve? Most of us would say steal the food. But instead of food, we were talking about love. We were talking about time. We were talking about attention. We were talking about life. How much of your life do you owe to your family and friends, and how much do you owe to the greater good?

Arthur Kleinman is a medical anthropologist who wrote a book about a similar issue: people who are caught between their own "ethical aspirations" on the one hand, and "society's moral reality" on the other. Often the values we aspire to are at odds with the world we live in.

The book is called *What Really Matters: Living a Moral Life Amidst Uncertainty and Danger*. In it, Kleinman tells the stories of a World War II vet who is haunted by the things he did under the guise of morality, of a Chinese man who makes ethical choices during the Cultural Revolution for which his family pays dearly, and of an aid worker in the Congo who is unsure whether the work she's done for decades will last. "How to live a moral life?" she asks. "I once thought I knew. I don't now."

In extreme social situations, this tension comes into sharper relief. But it contains the root from which all our dilemmas grow: our desire to be good to — or to be seen as good by — the people around us, and our desire to achieve a higher level of goodness.

"The book shows how we live in a world that is extraordinarily practical, uncertain, and dangerous," Kleinman said when I called to ask him about it, "and in that setting, we often make moral compromises. Ethics is frequently taught as black and white, but the world we live in is always gray."

In this gray world, our ethical choices are almost always a trade-off. But for us to know what we are trading, Kleinman says, you have to look at what people actually do rather than what they say. You must be aware of the values being lived versus the values being espoused. Only then, when you see the distance between what is and what should be, can you begin to explore what's at stake for yourself.

Maybe I'm exaggerating the import of that moment in my dorm room, but I remember it as a turning point, as the time when things began to grow less black and white for me. Being a good person suddenly didn't seem so simple. "Good to whom?" I started to wonder. "And good for what?" I began to see that there were many ways of being a good person, and that I was not being good to Bridgit. Sitting there after she left, I could see what was at stake for me.

I still have my solar panel, but I've never figured out how to use it. I recycle and compost, and I buy renewable energy credits. I used to volunteer as a tutor for refugees, and when my kids get a little older, I hope to do so again. Instead of writing letters, I write stories. I know these things are a far cry from leading the Salt March or defeating an empire through nonviolence. But after more than 20 years with Bridgit, I am also sure that it's one of the best trade-offs I've ever made.

December 2013

Free your mind: On creativity and genius

Spencer Silver lived just across town from where I sit typing this in Minneapolis. The 80-year-old chemist died recently. Silver's name may not be familiar to you, but his work has touched your life. And it offers lessons for all of us about what it means to be creative.

In the late 1960s, Silver was trying to come up with a strong glue that could be used in aircraft. Instead, he accidentally came up with the opposite: a weak glue that could be reused over and over.

Rather than seeing this as a failure, he saw the potential in his discovery. Silver promoted it within the company where he worked; for years, he gave talks about it. Finally, someone else came up with an application — a "reusable bookmark." But it was still several more years before the first Post-it Notes went on sale.

It was a creation that has, to some degree, changed the world.

The history of the Post-it Note challenges many of our beliefs about innovation, creativity, and even genius. When we think of those words, we might picture a lone inventor in a darkened room using the formidable powers of his or her mind to come up with something astonishing, something the world has never seen.

Silver was not like that. In fact, few creative people are. Craig Wright, author of *The Hidden Habits of Genius*, writes that a chemist colleague once told him, "Scientists don't have 'eureka' flashes. Rather, they experience 'My, that's strange' moments."

Wright is a musicologist who teaches a popular "genius course" at Yale University. He points out that geniuses often don't have high IQs or get perfect grades, and that their insights are often years, not seconds, in the making. "That 'aha' moment," he writes, "is really the culmination of a lengthy period of cerebral gestation."

He also notes that the core of creativity is not so much inventiveness as it is the ability to make connections. According to Wright, "the genius sees things others do not," a sentiment Steve Jobs echoed. "Creativity is just connecting things," he quotes Jobs as saying. "When you ask creative people how they did something, they feel a little guilty because they didn't really do it, they just saw something."

The ability to see new connections, to imagine things that aren't there, and to cast our minds into the future is the hallmark of our species and the reason for our success — at least that's what the anthropologist Agustín Fuentes argues in his book *The Creative Spark: How Imagination Made Humans Exceptional*. "Two million years ago," Fuentes writes, "our small, naked, fangless, hornless, and clawless ancestors with a few sticks and stones surmounted near-impossible odds. All because they had one another and a spark of creativity."

Fuentes continues that "no other animal in the wild, not even chimpanzees, can look at a rock, understand that inside that rock is another more useful shape, and use other rocks or wood or bone to modify that rock."

As a writer, I often feel a little like someone who is trying to peer inside a rock. Among the challenges of writing for a living, this is one that no one ever told me about: maintaining your creativity.

In certain industries, it has become popular to describe oneself as "a creative." But creativity, in my experience, is something that you attempt and, if you're lucky, achieve, rather than something that you are.

How does a person go about attempting creative work? In one sense, it simply entails coming up with something new. That's what the psychologist Mihaly Csikszentmihalyi calls "personal creativity," which can make life more interesting and meaningful.

But then there's "cultural creativity," which is when you contribute something new to your domain — whether it's art, science, or business — that somehow changes that domain. Geniuses are those who, by luck or circumstance, contribute something that changes the larger culture. "Innovation," meanwhile, could be defined as the ability to turn creativity into real-world products.

So the question is: How do we come up with new things?

In the early 1990s, Csikszentmihalyi conducted a yearslong study of 91 "exceptional individuals" — scientists, artists, and others who had made major contributions to their fields, including 14 Nobel Prize winners. They sat for extensive interviews on video that were later analyzed for common themes.

One thread that emerged was that measured intelligence is not a primary factor in creativity. In his book *Creativity: Flow and the Psychology of Discovery and Invention*, Csikszentmihalyi writes that IQ tests tend to measure "convergent thinking," or a person's ability to solve "well-defined, rational problems that have one correct answer." Creative people, on the other hand, engage in "divergent thinking," which involves the ability to think of many possible, but not strictly necessary, answers to a problem.

At the same time, Csikszentmihalyi says, you must be able to sort your good ideas from your bad ones. This has been a personal weak spot. I'm currently working on roughly four dozen stories and projects in some form. They all seemed AWESOME when I first came up with them.

They are not all awesome. I just can't quite tell which ones are worth saving until weeks, or sometimes years, later. During the pandemic lull, I culled my files, discarding notes on things I realized I would never write about — nanotechnology, nuclear fusion, and Mormon romance novels, to name a few.

Knowing what you don't want to create is a big step toward creating what you do want. But creativity isn't simply a matter of coming up with new ideas. According to Csikszentmihalyi, that's just one of five phases of creative work.

The first phase is what he calls *preparation*. In this stage, you immerse yourself in a particular problem or a field of knowledge. Then comes *incubation*, a mysterious process in which "ideas churn around below the threshold of consciousness." This is a key period in which your mind is not actively trying to solve the problem. In the best-case scenario, incubation leads to the third phase: *insight*. Wright, in a chapter titled "Now Relax," observed that painter Grant Wood said all his really good ideas came while he was milking a cow; Nikola Tesla thought of an electric motor — one that is still in use — while walking through a park reciting poetry with a friend; J.K. Rowling dreamed up Harry Potter while sitting on a train with nothing else to do.

But that only gets you partway there. Next comes *evaluation*, in which you decide whether your insight is worth keeping. Csikszentmihalyi calls this the most emotionally difficult part of the process. And finally, there's *elaboration*. This is the work, the 99 percent of genius that Thomas Edison spoke of. If you believe him, it means that the first four phases together make up just 1 percent of the process.

In reality, of course, creativity is never so neat as five distinct phases. It's messy and recursive and hard to control. But it's also how the world — and life — gets better. And there are things you can do to improve your odds of achieving something creative in your own life, in your work, or in your Rotary club.

In her book *Genius Unmasked*, Roberta Ness lists 11 "devices" used by scientific geniuses. These include finding the right question, observing, changing your point of view, broadening your perspective, and "frame shifting." Most of the devices involve attempting to see things differently. Wright also points out that "most invention comes from observing disparate things and seeing an unexpected relationship between them."

To do that, you have to find a balance between relaxation and concentration. Wright says you may need to erect an imaginary "fourth wall" against distractions and intrusions, like the one actors use on stage to separate themselves from their audience. If you want to be creative, first you have to create a space in which new ideas and connections can emerge. Csikszentmihalyi notes that "constant busyness is not a good prescription for creativity"; in fact, distraction and an inability to focus are some of the main obstacles. Creative people often devote much of their energy to protecting their attention, saving it for what they really want to spend it on.

"It takes a lot of time to be a genius," Gertrude Stein wrote. "You have to sit around so much, doing nothing, really doing nothing." In the end, the secret to being creative may not be the courage to do something new. It may have more to do with the courage not to do anything.

October 2021

Getting better all the time: On mastery

When I was in college, a favorite professor of mine gave me a thin yellow paperback. It was titled *Zen in the Art of Archery*. At first, I thought the author had borrowed the title from *Zen and the Art of Motorcycle Maintenance*. But it turned out to be the other way around.

Published in 1953, *Zen in the Art of Archery* told the story of a German philosopher named Eugen Herrigel, who'd lived in Japan between the world wars. During that time, he studied for six years under a master archer whose cryptic instructions about how to attain the proper frame of mind for hitting the target involved not worrying about hitting the target.

In the front of the book, my professor had inscribed, "In anticipation of the moment when 'the bowstring has cut right through you.'" This referred to a point in the book when Herrigel finally reaches a level of understanding about — a mastery of — himself and his shooting.

The inscription seemed to suggest that someday the bowstring would cut through me too. How would I know? What would it feel like? At the time I assumed it would probably happen when I hit the *New York Times* bestseller list or received my Nobel Prize. But I was missing the point entirely.

Over the years, I've thought a lot about that book and about Herrigel's progression from novice to accomplished archer. I thought about his frustration and failures as I encountered my own, and about how his progress seemed worthwhile not in spite of those setbacks, but because of them. This made sense: Discipline and persistence were the keys. Hard work would get you to the place where the bowstring cut through you.

Herrigel's message resonated throughout the 20th century, in books such as Robert M. Pirsig's *Zen and the Art of Motorcycle Maintenance* and Ray Bradbury's *Zen in the Art of Writing*, and in the lives of people such as George Leonard, an editor at *Look* magazine who became a leader in the so-called human potential movement of the 1970s. When Leonard was 47, he took up aikido and eventually became a fifth-degree black belt. He summed up his ideas in his 1992 book, *Mastery: The Keys to Success and Long-Term Fulfillment.*

Leonard identified five steps along this path: instruction, surrender, intentionality, something he called "the edge," and the most important, practice. "What is mastery?" he wrote. "At the heart of it, mastery is practice. Mastery is staying on the path."

He explained: "The people we know as masters don't devote themselves to their particular skill just to get better at it. The truth is, they love to practice — and because of this they do get better."

As I wrote more, the idea that the reward of mastery comes from the process of getting there seemed more and more true. I would find myself most content when I was working hard at something, so engrossed in it that everything else fell away. It was from these times that my best work emerged. This was a state of mind that psychology researcher Mihaly Csikszentmihalyi calls "flow." He has noted that the best word to describe this state is "enjoyment," which comes from the practice itself — it is intrinsic. ("Pleasure," meanwhile, is extrinsic.) As Nobel Prize-winning author Naguib Mahfouz told him: "I love my work more than I love what it produces."

"Being an engineer or a carpenter is not in itself enjoyable," Csikszentmihalyi wrote. "But if one does these things a certain way, then they become intrinsically rewarding, worth doing for their own sake."

This tension between enjoyment and pleasure, between intrinsic and extrinsic motivations, is a paradox at the heart of mastering anything. These days, we are often drawn toward extrinsic metrics of success. But if you don't learn to love the practice, you won't get very far — or if you do, it will be more of a forced march than a rewarding journey. In this journey, Herrigel observed, "practice, repetition, and repetition of the repeated with ever-increasing intensity are its distinctive features for long stretches of the way."

In his book *Outliers*, Malcolm Gladwell highlighted the notion that to become an expert at anything, you must devote at least 10,000 hours to it. But neither Gladwell nor anyone else talks much about what it takes to be able to (or to want to) put in 10,000 hours. "Mastery is not a function of genius or talent," wrote business writer Robert Greene in his 2012 book *Mastery*. "It is a function of time and intense focus applied to a particular field of knowledge." But for Greene (who advocates 20,000 hours), mastery is "a form of dominance and power" that can lead you to the top of your field. For him, mastery is about winning.

Maybe it was for me too, at one point — back when my professor handed me that book. But I've had plenty of time to think about what happens when you devote yourself to something, about persistence, and about learning to enjoy what you do. For example, Csikszentmihalyi wrote that of the 91 "exceptional individuals" he interviewed for his book *Creativity* — many of whom had won Nobel Prizes or attained similar status — "all agree that they do what they do primarily because it's fun."

I still don't know exactly what Herrigel meant about the bowstring cutting right though you. And, as I discovered in working on this column, he may not have either: In 2001, Japanese scholar Yamada Shoji published a paper (and more recently a book) arguing that Herrigel's insights were more the result of cultural and linguistic misinterpretations than of a philosopher's steps toward enlightenment.

In one instance, when Herrigel's instructor fired two arrows across a darkened room and the second arrow split the first one in two, the instructor stared at it in silence, which Herrigel interpreted as a profound moment of meditation. But according to Shoji, it was considered shameful to damage one's own equipment, so he was probably thinking something more like, "Darn, my arrow!" Elsewhere, the instructor appears to have told Herrigel, "It shoots," after a particularly good shot, which the philosopher interpreted as a mystical statement about Zen. Shoji notes that the Japanese phrase actually meant, quite simply, "Nice shot."

Years ago, I would have found this disturbing, perhaps even devastating. But I see now that, even if *Zen in the Art of Archery* wasn't really about Zen, it was about archery. It was about practice. And in that sense, it was about everything.

As for the bowstring cutting right though me, I'm sure that rather than being the result of hard work, that moment is the hard work. It's the simple joy of being absorbed by something you love doing; of forgetting about everything but the arrow, the target, and the bow; and of one day, to your surprise, discovering that you are better at it than you used to be, even if you still have a long way to go.

July 2013

Sage coach: On finding wisdom

Recently I was looking through some of my grandmother's things and came across her tattered, softcover Bible. As I paged through it, a yellowed newspaper article fell out. It was from a 1966 edition of the *Minneapolis Star*, written by a certain Dr. Walter C. Alvarez. It was titled "You Can Grow Old Gracefully. "

Nowadays, that sentiment is not very widespread. Growing old has become something to be dreaded, feared, and, if possible, avoided. This is partly rooted in America's youth-oriented culture, which differs from that of places like Japan or parts of Africa, where older people are seen as repositories of wisdom and authority.

Still, I liked the headline of Dr. Alvarez's column, even if the useful advice in his article was limited to exhortations to read widely, be friendly, and try to cultivate an interesting persona in youth and middle age. If you become a good and interesting person when you're young, he wrote, you will be a good and interesting person when you are old.

My grandmother did, in fact, age gracefully. She never become bitter or isolated or hopeless, even though her husband died — after falling off a ladder — just four years after she cut out that article. For as long as she could manage, she played bridge, went to water aerobics, and worked the crossword puzzle, and she always seemed able to see the humor in things. That she kept that article — in her Bible no less — meant that she must have had some faith that aging gracefully was something she could do.

So do I. I'm now coasting through middle age, ever closer to the time when I am clearly "growing old" — a phrase I prefer in that, unlike "getting old," it implies that aging is a process in which you can play some part, rather than something that simply happens to you.

But if Dr. Alvarez was correct that the kind of young person you are, or were, is also the kind of old person you will be, I could be out of luck. I have seldom felt as though I am living gracefully. But I'm not ready to give up yet on becoming a wise older person. Fortunately I have role models, like Bernie Otis, a member of the Rotary Club of Woodland Hills, California, and a popular speaker at clubs around those parts. He is 88, has a bad leg, and lives in a senior home. None of that has slowed him down.

"Life does not stop until you stop living it," he said when I called him. "And no matter how old you are, or what impairment you have, if you have knowledge about something, if your brain is working, then you have something to contribute to society. You can do things and help people."

I had gotten a note from Otis about a book he had written titled *How to Prepare for Old Age (Without Taking the Fun Out of Life)*, which mixes his observations with some practical advice about getting older. (And in which, full disclosure, he quotes from a few of my *Rotarian* columns.) Otis spent his career designing hotel restaurants in Las Vegas and still has an active presence on LinkedIn, where he writes about sales and marketing and offers free phone consultations. (He recently helped two former colleagues get jobs working on Apple's new campus food complex.) He just took a position on the board of the Glendale International Film Festival. Mostly he focuses on giving back from his own store of knowledge and experience.

"So many people who are living in senior homes are fully capable," Otis says. "They have knowledge. They have the ability to do things. But they're not setting any new goals for themselves. They're not planning anything. Life is about creating opportunities for yourself. If you have knowledge about something, find the people who could use that knowledge. There isn't a day that goes by that I'm not doing something that's helping people. And I'm loving it."

Otis is describing what psychologist Erik Erikson called "generativity," which is a sense that you are contributing to society, to the next generation, or to the future. It's something that becomes important later in life — after we find love, after we find work, after we find our identity and our place in society. Having children is one way we do that, but there are many others, all of which contribute to what psychologists call "eudemonic" well-being. That term refers to the amount of meaning in your life — as opposed to "hedonic" well-being, or the amount of pleasure you feel.

A talent for that kind of big-picture thinking is one key to aging gracefully, though it can be hard to achieve, let alone maintain. (I suspect Otis may have always had it.) And while there is no precise criteria for what makes a person "wise," other abilities might include recognizing the limits of your own knowledge, being able to see others' perspectives, seeking out compromise, regulating your emotions, understanding that change is inevitable, and being aware that events may unfold in different ways. Researchers sometimes distinguish between kinds of wisdom — benevolent, philosophical, and practical — but they agree that wisdom is different from intelligence. You can be smart but not wise.

One universal assumption about wisdom (with apologies to Dr. Alvarez) is that it increases with age. But in fact, this seems to vary by culture. A few years ago, Igor Grossmann, director of the Wisdom and Culture Lab at the University of Waterloo in Canada, conducted a study in which he found that Americans' ability to reason wisely — including being able to recognize other people's perspectives, the limits of one's personal knowledge, and the importance of compromise — does, in fact, grow as they get older. But in Japan it stays about the same, since even young people there are likely to use those strategies.

Grossmann is one of a few scientists researching the boundaries of wisdom. He points out that self-help books about how to become wise are as numerous as those advising how to become happy and healthy, but that none are based on data.

Now that Grossmann and others are gathering that data, it seems inevitable that more of our assumptions will fall. Another one is that wisdom is a quality, a personality trait, or a state that we arrive at and don't leave. According to Grossmann, wisdom is best seen as situational.

"The lay belief about wisdom is that either you have it or you don't, and that wise people are always wise and the majority of us are not wise," he says. "But that is not really what happens. What happens is that all of us have some distribution of wisdom from one situation to the next. And there's great variability. There's actually more variability within people than between people: You can be super wise and yet vary dramatically from situation A to situation B."

That's the bad news: There is no free ride on the wisdom train. But the good news is that Grossmann and others have found ways to increase wise reasoning in a given situation, through "self-distancing" or looking at a situation from an outsider's perspective. One strategy is to explain that situation to an imaginary 12-year-old. Another is to visualize yourself from a bird's-eye view. Another is to refer to yourself — out loud — in the third person.

"These strategies make people less self-centered," Grossmann says. "And they are pretty effective for boosting wisdom — things like talking to yourself in the third person before making an important decision. Ask, 'What would Frank do?' instead of, 'What would I do?'"

Over the next few days, I tried this. Although it felt a little strange at first, it didn't seem as megalomaniacal as I thought it would. In fact, my thinking was cooler, clearer, more removed. I was surprised how powerful the shift was and how much it felt as though I was watching the person I wanted to be. I became less afraid of things not going my way. I felt more open to whatever might unfold. It became easier to see from others' point of view.

This wasn't quite wisdom yet, but I hope it was the beginning of it. Maybe there's still time for me to grow old a little more gracefully and a little more wisely.

June 2017

STORIES

Past imperfect: On having room to grow

In the early days of Facebook, one of my high school classmates started posting photos from parties that we had attended back in the 1980s. Until then, I was unaware that these pictures even existed. My classmate scanned them, posted them, then tagged everyone. They were not compromising or embarrassing — they were just pictures of us standing around, looking as bored and awkward as I remember us being.

For some of my classmates, this might have been a pleasant trip down memory lane. For me it was unsettling, although I couldn't put my finger on why.

There are many reasons I'm glad Facebook didn't exist when I was growing up. I held opinions that I've since disavowed. I made jokes that were embarrassing or offensive. Often, I did not take the high road. I accept that I did these things, but mostly I'm glad they are in the past, lodged behind a wall of forgetfulness. I'm glad my permanent record has been allowed to lapse.

But what if it hadn't? What if everything you ever did or said was ready to be called up as evidence, forever? The reappearance of photos from a forgotten part of my life was a sign of a profound change in how we live in the world. It pointed to a future when your past trails behind you like a chain that can never be cut. It signaled the arrival of an era when your history, your mistakes, your poor choices, your party pictures will forever weigh you down.

When I was young, the past disappeared quickly, even inevitably, unless someone made an effort to preserve it. A friend's dad owned a camcorder and carried a huge backpack full of video equipment. He would run around recording everything; we thought this was absurd. We called him "Captain Video."

But today we are all Captain Video, gleefully, even recklessly, recording our lives. Maybe it's progress: It makes us think harder about the things we say and the choices we make, because we know they may be there forever.

But I also wonder if this is why young people are reported to have an obsession with self-improvement that their parents lack: For them, the pressure to be (or to appear to be) their best selves never relents. This may be creating a generation of people who are better behaved, but also more cautious and less willing to make the kinds of mistakes that can help a person grow. To be clear: I'm not talking about committing crimes or serious transgressions. I'm talking about foolishness, youth, identity, phases.

There are many reasons I'm glad Facebook didn't exist when I was growing up. I held opinions that I've since disavowed. I made jokes that were embarrassing or offensive. Often, I did not take the high road.

Recently I came across an essay by writer David Quammen titled "The Siphuncle." It's about the nautilus, an ancient, predatory shellfish.

Every month or two, Quammen wrote, the nautilus moves up toward the entrance of its shell, secreting a pearl-like substance called nacre to seal off the chamber behind it. In this wall of pearl, it leaves a small hole for an organ called a siphuncle, through which it moves water in and out of the chambers in order to float up or down. These chambers allow the nautilus to control its path through the ocean in search of prey.

Woven into this natural history is Quammen's story of his own walled-off past. When he was younger, he was obsessed with William Faulkner, whose books he tried to translate into film scripts. He wrote an unpublishable novel about Faulkner's death. He even got a job working on a doomed documentary about Faulkner in the writer's hometown.

When that job ended, so did that phase of his life. He saw where the Faulknerian path was leading — toward academia — and he turned away. "I evaded the looming Volvo and the corduroy jacket with leather elbows and the unfunny early marriage," Quammen wrote. So he sealed that phase behind its own wall and went on to become one of the great science writers and essayists of his generation.

The idea of reinventing oneself is one of the core tenets of the modern world, especially the American one. Immigrants came to places such as the United States and Canada to start over, to become someone different, to make a new life. Many of them would never see their homelands again. The same was true for the pioneers who went west.

Once you crossed the ocean or the Rocky Mountains, you could become someone else. You could leave the past behind.

Until fairly recently, this was still the case for most of us, even if we never left our hometowns: Our past was there, but we could bring it to the surface or let it sink as needed. We could try on new identities, new lives, new ideas, new selves and know that we might also grow out of them. If you wanted to leave your old self behind, you could move to Alaska. But really, all you had to do was wait.

An example: When I was in my 20s, I was a die-hard "anarcho-syndicalist" and an acolyte of linguist and political writer Noam Chomsky. I read endlessly about the Spanish Civil War and wrote about "industrial democracy." I dreamed of a world where we all were free to make the good choices we would surely make if there were no government. Now I find those beliefs slightly embarrassing, but I am not forced to relive them every day. Instead, I am free to look back on my younger self with a mixture of mortification and compassion.

The chambers of our lives are never as neat as those of the nautilus. And often it's only when we're on the other side that their worth becomes clear. That's when we can hold them up and inspect them like fossils from our personal evolution.

I have changed my mind many times about many things. I have always believed that we can learn from our mistakes, that we can grow, that we can move on. I think that's why seeing those old photos on Facebook was so unsettling. The implication was that I was still that person. And in a sense that was true. But in another sense, it was not.

For people whose youth predates the internet, our pasts may no longer remain safely behind the walls we've built. Younger people may never get to build those walls in the first place. The idea of a many-chambered life now seems as prehistoric as the nautilus.

We all have to find a way to live in a world where the past is ever-present, where our online lives become our permanent record — the one that employers, colleges, friends, lovers, neighbors, children, and even the law can sift through to see who we were, regardless of who we are. Even if I delete my account, somewhere, on a server beyond my control, my past lives on.

Some days all this makes me want to run for the hills. Instead, I'm trying to learn to accept the phases I've gone through and the people I've been. And I am trying to make the same allowance for those around me — the people they've been and the people they might still become. Because we all need room to grow, to change, and to chart our own course through these waters we are swimming in together.

June 2018

Braking news: On headlines and head space

In 1986, a man named Christopher Knight walked into the Maine woods and found an isolated spot to pitch a tent. He remained there until 2013, when he was caught stealing food from a summer camp. In all those years, the man known as the North Pond Hermit never talked to another person. His world was limited to his immediate surroundings.

When journalist Michael Finkel interviewed Knight for his book *The Stranger in the Woods: The Extraordinary Story of the Last True Hermit*, he asked Knight what he thought of the changes in technology since he had removed himself from contact with the modern world. Knight was unimpressed. "People earnestly say to me here, 'Mr. Knight, we have cell phones now, and you're going to really enjoy them.' That's their enticement for me to rejoin society. … I have no desire. And what about a text message? Isn't that just using a telephone as a telegraph? We're going backwards."

After Knight dropped out of society, there was a revolution in the way we get news: Every hour of every day, messages and alerts arrive in our computers and our phones. Most of us accept this as progress. But for 27 years, Knight existed in a bubble, even as the rest of us became more and more enmeshed in the flow of news speeding into our lives. We now spend an average of 11 hours a day "interacting with media," staring at our screens and reading about things happening far away.

In and of itself, this is not a bad thing. We need to be informed in order to help others who might need it. Yet there is a cost to this nonstop influx of news. Constantly monitoring the news can affect our emotional state, our energy level, our mental health, and even our worldview.

Knight has likely never suffered from the condition known as headline stress disorder, or news fatigue. But many of us have: According to a 2019 survey by the American Psychological Association, 54 percent of people said that following the news causes them stress. And a 2018 study by the Pew Research Center found that 68 percent of Americans feel "exhausted" by their news consumption.

Among the many reasons that too much news might not be good for you, the most significant is that news tends to be more negative than the world really is. We have an innate need to pay attention to bad news, because, in evolutionary terms, such information can be more important to our immediate survival. Scientists call this our "negativity bias."

We all know how hard it is to turn away from stories about terror attacks, hurricanes, shipwrecks, dying coral reefs, or whatever the disaster might be. But when we consume these stories continuously, it takes a serious toll on us. In 2015, researchers in Israel found that "increased frequency of viewing newscasts" causes a jump in "uncontrolled fear, physiological hyperarousal, sleeping difficulties, and fearful thoughts" and makes a person 1.6 times more likely to experience at least one symptom of anxiety.

Psychologists Wendy Johnston and Graham Davey conducted another study, in which participants watched 14-minute segments of positive, negative, or neutral news. The viewers of negative news reported being more anxious and sad afterward than the two other groups. But the effect didn't stop there. It carried over into concerns about the participants' own lives, making them more likely to "catastrophize" personal concerns that had nothing to do with the news. As Davey writes, "not only are negatively valenced news broadcasts likely to make you sadder and more anxious, they are also likely to exacerbate your own personal worries and anxieties."

These days, negative news is all around us. It's in our pockets. It's in our cars. It's in the waiting room. We live in an ocean of bad stories, so it's no wonder many of us feel we are being swept away. Some 69 percent of Americans report that worrying about the future of the nation causes them stress. This is at a time when by many measures — education, income, life expectancy — we've never been better off.

In the past, news wasn't so immediate. By the time we read it in the paper, some time had passed, which allowed for a healthy feeling of distance. Much of what we read about today is also distant from us, in that it doesn't affect our daily lives. Paying undue heed can make us blind to many of the things that do matter.

This is not a new insight. In 1854, another would-be hermit named Henry David Thoreau put down similar sentiments in *Walden*, which he wrote while living in a cabin on a pond. In the book, he complained about our appetite for a constant influx of news.

"Hardly a man takes a half hour's nap after dinner, but when he wakes he holds up his head and asks, 'What's the news?' as if the rest of mankind had stood his sentinels," he wrote, adding, "I am sure that I never read any memorable news in a newspaper."

Thoreau's position was extreme. He eschewed the news not because he wasn't interested, but because he didn't want to be distracted from the things that he thought mattered. "I went to the woods," he famously stated, "because I wished to live deliberately, to front only the essential facts of life."

The question for us is: Which facts are the essential ones? Is it knowing exactly which politicians are up in the polls, or that a building has burned down, or whether a hurricane has made landfall? It's no wonder we have trouble appreciating the simple pleasures our life has to offer.

When I think back to my own best days, times that seem truly joyful, they are times when past tragedies and future disasters didn't seem to matter: a sunny picnic with my wife in a New Zealand vineyard; holding my newborn daughter for the first time; playing soccer with friends in a park in Italy; skipping rocks on Lake Superior with my girls. In those times, I was just there.

None of which is to say that we shouldn't read the news. But to let tomorrow's worries overwhelm today's joys is a bad bargain. To save the future, first we need to save the present.

"Let us spend one day as deliberately as Nature," Thoreau wrote, "and not be thrown off the track by every nutshell and mosquito's wing that falls on the rails."

You don't have to hide in the woods to do that. All you need to do is spend one day without the news. By the end of it, I can guarantee, the world will already feel a little better.

February 2020

Could be worse: On declinism and redemption

Late last year a woman I know tweeted: "Great — subzero temps next week. Let's just get this out there — 2016 has been the worst year ever!"

Honestly, I wasn't crazy about 20 below zero either, but in Minnesota, putting on a jacket and hat hardly seems like the end of civilization. More recently, I saw another post on Twitter in which the writer said, "I'm just always mad now. Everything is garbage and it doesn't need to be."

The idea that 2016 was the worst year ever started circulating after several celebrity deaths (Prince, David Bowie, Leonard Cohen) were followed by an election that did not go the way many people wanted it to. After that, the worst-year-ever meme became unstoppable, and in 2017, the drumbeat of decline has not stopped.

Offhand, I can think of a lot of things that are worse than a cold winter day: the 2004 Indian Ocean tsunami, the 1929 stock market crash, the Bataan Death March. But it's true that things do feel worse than they actually are. Part of the reason lies in the 24-hour news cycle and its never-ending flow of bad news. As writer Jia Tolentino put it in *The New Yorker*, "There is no limit to the amount of misfortune a person can take in via the internet, and there's no easy way to properly calibrate it. … Our ability to change things is not increasing at the same rate as our ability to know about them."

Whatever the reason, the downbeat trend has accelerated among people of all political stripes, and it is noteworthy because it goes directly against the strongest current in American culture: our optimism, our sense that problems are meant to be solved and that solving them is our job. Since our country's founding, America has been a can-do place, a place of possibility. Our creed has always been a certain sometimes naive faith that things will work out for the best. And for the most part — believe it or not — they have.

Contrary to what you might think, violence is at all-time lows, as is the rate of global poverty. War deaths are fewer than ever in history. On most indicators where you might think progress is not being made, the opposite is probably true. Nicholas Kristof recently pointed out in a column in *The New York Times*: "2017 is likely to be the best year in the history of humanity." He continued: "Every day, another 250,000 people graduate from extreme poverty, according to World Bank figures. About 300,000 get electricity for the first time. Some 285,000 get their first access to clean drinking water. When I was a boy, a majority of adults had always been illiterate, but now more than 85 percent can read."

Likewise, in 2011 Steven Pinker pointed out in *The Better Angels of Our Nature* that the world is not more violent, more racist, more genocidal, or more unjust than in the past. He documented long-term declines in homicides, war deaths, executions, and lynchings, as well as massive gains in education, health, and wealth. He showed that diseases are not spiraling out of control. And humanity is not (yet) devolving into a Hobbesian state of nature. None of which is to say that things are perfect or that our progress is permanent. But the world is far more perfect than it used to be.

Yet many of us have given in to a pessimism, a hopelessness, a sense that things are going from bad to worse. Minnesota winters notwithstanding, it was shocking how many people rushed to declare 2016 the worst year ever, when in fact it was one of the best.

This disconnect between perception and reality was noted by sociologist Barry Glassner in his 1999 book *The Culture of Fear: Why Americans Are Afraid of the Wrong Things*. In it he explored the growing distance between the things we fear and the reality of those threats. Throughout the 1990s, people became more afraid of crime, even as crime rates were falling. Some threats, such as road rage and child abduction, proved wildly overblown, while others — the satanic cult scare and Y2K, for instance — turned out to be entirely fictional.

Why this divergence? Why don't we see things as they are? Glassner attributed this in part to "premillennial tensions." But now the turn of the millennium is long past, yet the tensions remain.

Another explanation is that this growing sense of decline is caused by something within us. Humans, as scientist and writer E.O. Wilson has observed, are the storytelling species. When we think about the past, we do not think in a steady stream of time. Rather, we think in terms of "episodes" that we link together, each one causing the next, like dominoes. This is true whether we are thinking about our life, our country, or our planet.

Psychologists who study these things have identified patterns in the stories we see. In American culture, the dominant kind are "redemption stories," in which a person faces loss, challenge, or difficulty, but overcomes it so that good emerges in the end. In his book *The Redemptive Self: Stories Americans Live By*, psychologist Dan McAdams argued that telling redemptive stories about oneself is linked to helping others. The opposite of redemptive stories are "contamination stories" in which things start out well, then something bad happens, after which everything goes from bad to worse. The end.

In a fascinating study called "The Political Is Personal: Narrating 9/11 and Psychological Well-Being," psychologists Jonathan Adler and Michael Poulin investigated why some people see redemption where others see contamination. They took accounts of nearly 400 people written two months after the 11 September 2001 attacks. They analyzed these stories and compared them against the results of those subjects' physical and mental health questionnaires. What they found was that people whose stories of 9/11 included themes of redemption and closure also had higher levels of psychological well-being and lower levels of distress. People whose stories of 9/11 were high in contamination — something bad happened, then everything was garbage — showed higher levels of internal distress and lower levels of psychological well-being. In other studies, Adler found that redemption stories were linked to improvements in mental health over the next few years, while contamination stories were not.

In other words, the stories we tell ourselves matter, and what we see around us often says more about our inner world than our outer one. "There's nothing objective about a contamination sequence," Adler told me. "All lives have positive and negative things that happen in them. But it's about how you parse time and draw connections."

Does this matter? Does it affect anyone but the storyteller? The answer is yes: Stories are contagious, and negative stories even more so. But I think it matters for other reasons too. One reason is that a negative outlook doesn't let us acknowledge the accomplishments of those who are doing good work: people fighting to eliminate polio, or end child marriage, or combat global warming, or conserve our water, or educate our children.

But the most important reason that we shouldn't let contamination narratives infect the rest of our stories is the simple fact that no problem has ever been solved by people who didn't think it was possible to solve it. When we let the negative memes take over — when we consume them over and over online — they create a cage of despair from which we can't see an escape. And this poses a real danger when it comes to problems such as climate change. It is a problem we can solve, as long as we don't allow the "worst year ever" meme to become a self-fulfilling prophecy.

But we can influence both the stories we see and the stories we tell. "One of the empowering insights from the field of narrative psychology," says Adler, "is that we are both the main character in our story and the narrator. So most of the day we go around being the main character, doing the stuff of our life. But when we need to, we can step out of being the main character and be the narrator — and revise the story if it's not working for us."

This is not always easy, but it is possible. So when the flood of bad news threatens to wash us away, remember that things are better than they seem. Step away from the flow of despair before it ruins not only your present, but your future. Look around you and write a new story that reflects the world as you want it to be.

November 2017

In search of a storied past: On family and history

My dad and I were on our way south, moving through rolling farmland. The sun was bright and the fields were green. It felt as though we were in a Grant Wood painting, caught between the smallness of our lives and the grandness of the sky. High above, stark white clouds cast shadows on the highway.

"Are we in Iowa yet?" I asked.

"We've been in Iowa for quite a while," he responded.

"Do you want me to look at the map?"

"If you want to."

We were also headed back in time, on a rescue mission of sorts. With me I had an audio recorder and a bunch of questions. For several years, I had been researching and writing about stories — about the way we use them to stitch ourselves together with the world around us. But I didn't have a full picture of my own family's story. I was sure I could find more pieces that would help me trace the links in the chain leading from my life into the past.

I had come across some fascinating studies on family stories and the power they have over us. In recent years, researchers have noted that children in families that eat dinner together often have better emotional health and are happier and more resilient than their peers. This has less to do with eating together than it does with the fact that family dinners provide space for stories to emerge. And knowing your family stories can make a real difference in your life.

Researchers asked adolescents questions such as, "Do you know where your parents met?" "Do you know where your grandparents grew up?" "Do you know of something terrible that happened in your family?"

Those who know the answers to more of those questions, says developmental psychologist Robyn Fivush, "show higher self-esteem, fewer behavior problems, and more resilience in the face of difficulties." This may be because knowing those things gives them more tools to deal with what life holds in store for them.

"Adolescents are facing the challenge of figuring out who they are in the world," Fivush says. "Why am I the person I am? How did I become this way? And a lot of that is about the family I came from. Adolescents use those stories to create models of how the world should look, what a person should be like. We think adolescents are not listening. But they are. They really want these stories."

Growing up, I knew some stories from my mom's side of the family but few from my dad's, other than that they came from what is now the Czech Republic and that occasionally we would eat pastries filled with enough poppy seeds to fail a drug test.

Over the years I had tried to get him to tell me some family stories. But his accounts were disjointed and hard to follow. In terms Fivush and others use, they lacked narrative "coherence."

"Coherence" is a tricky term, but in general it means that earlier episodes in a family's story *cause* the later ones. "The critical component of coherence is that it's a story that makes human sense," Fivush says. "It explains human motivations, intentions, and actions." In other words, such stories tell us why people did things and what happened as a result.

People with more coherent stories about themselves or their families have higher levels of both physical and psychological health. Conversely, depressed people have trouble telling coherent stories, though it's not clear whether depression causes stories to become incoherent or whether incoherent stories contribute to depression.

"How do you feel about going back?" I asked.

"Oh, fine. When you get there, lots of memories come back that are buried," he said. "There are good things."

I was hoping some of those memories would help me start putting together a more cohesive picture. I knew there were some good things, but I knew more about the bad ones: My grandma was depressed and took her own life a few years before I was born. For many years, my dad — her only child — felt responsible. And I didn't learn any of that until I was an adult.

Late in the morning, we rolled into Cedar Rapids, a town once filled with Czech immigrants. Today there is still a "Czech Village," a Czech museum, and a century-old Czech bakery, but most of the Czech speakers are gone.

As we drove around town, looking at houses he remembered, recalling aunts and uncles he loved, he talked about "Grampa Hermanek" (meaning his mom's grandfather) who had been in the Prussian emperor's honor guard, until one night there was a fight and someone was killed. He and his wife escaped to Vienna and made their way across Europe, selling the clothes that had been her dowry along the way. They sailed to New York, then headed for Chicago, which had a large Czech community. After a few years, they took a covered wagon to South Dakota to homestead, but quit and came back east to Cedar Rapids, where they could speak their own language.

"In the Hermanek house, my mother and her aunt Emily, who was like a sister, used to go out quite a bit at night," my dad said. "Grampa Hermanek didn't like that and said they should stay home. He called them *kurva*, which means 'whore' in Czech."

I hadn't known that, and as I heard these details, I could feel them falling into a kind of order. Their journey had not been an easy one; it was full of hardships and failures as well as some successes. Although there were good times, my grandma's life, in many respects, was tragic. And according to Marshall Duke, a professor of psychology at Emory University, this is important, because not all family stories are created equal: Some have more power than others.

Duke divides family stories into three kinds: First are the *ascending* stories, in which a family comes from nothing and succeeds. Then there are the *descending*, in which a family experiences hardship, failure, or loss. Last are what he calls the *oscillating* stories, in which a family's fortunes rise and fall. These seem to afford the most benefit to later generations of listeners.

"It helps kids realize that there are ups and downs in life, and that the family they belong to has experienced both ups and downs and overcome the downs," says Duke. "That's a good message: If something is going badly, it's happened before, and we'll be OK."

I am probably past the age where I could gain much from such stories. I still liked hearing them; they made my own problems feel small. But the real benefit of knowing your family's story may be even more basic.

"It seems to give you a sense of grounding," says Duke, "a sense of belonging to something larger than yourself, something that has lasted longer than you have lasted. The 10-year-old learns not just about the past 10 years, but the past 60 or 100 years. It's an ownership of a history that you are both responsible for carrying, as well as continuing."

We drove one day to the National Czech & Slovak Museum & Library, where we learned that for many people, "the Czech and Slovak journey" started when feudalism was abolished in the Austro-Hungarian Empire after 1848 and the first wave of immigrants from those lands came to the United States. We visited a humble late-1800s immigrant house, probably not unlike the one Grandpa Hermanek lived in.

I asked for information about our family, and the librarian came back with a "Bures Family History" pamphlet compiled in 1971 — the year I was born, and 110 years after Jiří Bureš arrived on a farm southeast of Cedar Rapids — where the "Buresh Cemetery" is still located.

Here was a tangible link, a direct line from the old world to my world, stretching back over 150 years. As we walked around, as I collected pieces of the past, I could feel them being woven into a line that felt stronger, thicker, more complete, more real. After all, isn't that why we seek out our family stories in old ledgers and even our DNA? To trace our connection to something larger than just ourselves: to history, to humanity?

We left the museum and walked down the street to the Czech Village and stopped in the Village Meat Market & Cafe for lunch, where we ordered schnitzel and goulash and talked while we ate.

"When you think about all the Czech people in Cedar Rapids, do you feel like you are still part of that?"

"Yes," he said. "I'm a piece of it."

We left the restaurant and bought some poppy-seed pastries at the bakery across the street. Then we went back to the car and headed out of town. As we drove away, I could feel the past pulling at me in a way I never had before: For the first time, I felt I was a piece of it too.

October 2018

Open to interpretation: On books, language, and cultures

Whenever I arrive in a new country, one of the first places I go is a bookstore. I do this for several reasons. Having spent much of my life and income in them, I always find them to be comforting spaces. And they often stock more specific maps and guides than you can get outside the country.

But the real reason I love these places is that by scanning the titles for sale — just gazing down the spines — I can get a glimpse of how people in that country see themselves. What stories do they tell? What stories do they read? What books do they print? And what do they import from abroad? And though this is harder in countries where I don't speak the language, I go anyway. Sometimes you can tell what genres are selling — what that country's readers want to know and what they aspire to be.

I've experienced almost every corner of the book industry: I have bought and read and loved books, of course. I have sorted and sold them at one of the world's largest bookstores. I've scouted them at rummage sales to sell myself. For a few months I worked in a book recycling factory, where we chopped up 30,000 pounds of books a day — titles like Zsa Zsa Gabor's *One Lifetime Is Not Enough* and Shirley MacLaine's *Going Within*. Their pages were then bound into massive bales that went on to be reborn as other things (with luck, more books). Most recently, I wrote a book myself.

That may be why I've never put much stock in the technophiles and futurists who've been predicting the end of printed books since the dawn of the internet. Today, the end of books seems further away than ever: Total printed book sales rose 2.4 percent in 2014 and 2.8 percent in 2015. In her own book, *The World between Two Covers: Reading the Globe*, writer Ann Morgan notes that the University Library at Cambridge adds roughly 500 books to its collection every day — one every 2.88 minutes.

In 2009, 500,000 English-language books were published worldwide. But very few non- English books are translated into our language. In 2008 in the UK and Ireland, only 4.37 percent of the literary works published were translations, according to Morgan. She began to wonder about all the books and stories that she was missing, and she decided to take on a methodical and audacious project: to spend a year reading a book from every country on the planet.

This presented several problems. First, how many countries are there? This might seem like a simple matter, but it's not. The number usually cited is 196, including Taiwan. But as Morgan points out in her book, some 270 national flags are flying around the world, and 280 country-code internet domains are recognized by ICANN, the authority on such things. There are places such as Western Sahara, Gibraltar, and Palestine — places whose residents feel they live in their own country, but whose more powerful neighbors may not. The question of what a country is can be tricky.

Other problems also arose: How do you pick a single book to represent a country? Which book will best capture the spirit of a country or its people? And how do you determine exactly what country a particular book is from? Is V.S. Naipaul English or Trinidadian? Is Junot Díaz's *The Brief Wondrous Life of Oscar Wao* an American book or a Dominican one? Is *American Gods*, a science fiction account by English-born Neil Gaiman about the various deities brought to this continent an American book, an English one, or something else?

Then there are the countries that have produced hardly any books at all: For the tiny state of San Marino, which sits within the borders of Italy, Morgan had to settle for a history, *The Republic of San Marino*. For Guinea-Bissau in West Africa, the only English-language book she could find was a collection of speeches and writing by independence leader Amílcar Cabral called *Unity and Struggle*. For a book from Mozambique, Morgan contacted a defunct company to get an unpublished translation of *Ualalapi* by Ungulani Ba Ka Khosa, which is considered one of the great African novels of the 20th century and which has never been published in English. The island nation of São Tomé and Príncipe had no English-language books at all, so Morgan bought several Portuguese copies of Olinda Beja's *The Shepherd's House*, found nine people willing to translate chapters, and ended up with a brand new book of her own.

Such literary spelunking can be exhilarating, and Morgan laments the fact that we all don't do more of it. But even if more books were translated, would more be read?

Many of the books that I love — Kenyan writer Ngugi wa Thiong'o's *Matigari*, Nigerian author Chris Abani's *GraceLand*, Ugandan writer Doreen Baingana's *Tropical Fish* — are fun for me because I've spent time in those places. I can remember the sounds and the voices. Reading those books is like going back for a visit. I have been to the bookshops there and pulled the books off the shelf myself, then walked out into the streets they describe. I can recall the sounds and voices surrounding the stories that unfold in their pages.

Every book is a kind of journey. And just as when we board a plane for a country we've never been to, a book from a new place contains the thrill of not knowing what you will find when you arrive. "Page by page," Morgan writes, "these regions ... became living, breathing entities, as if their stories had made them real."

That is what books do: They make our stories real, physical. They turn our ideas into tangible things. They are like rafts where we put the things we believe in and hope for. Then we push them out to sea.

Perhaps that's why, when Morgan announced her project, people from around the world rushed to offer suggestions and help with translations. Some even sent her books from their local shops, in the hope that their stories could cross over into the larger world.

In his dystopian novel *Fahrenheit 451*, Ray Bradbury imagined a world where books were so powerful the government sent its "firemen" to burn them because they threatened the world it wanted to exist.

One character, looking back, recalls: "Books were ... where we stored a lot of things we were afraid we might forget. There is nothing magical in them, at all. The magic is only in what books say, how they stitched the patches of the universe together into one garment for us."

July 2016

Pomp and happenstance: On graduation and life

It's possible that future anthropologists will look back on our civilization and conclude that all our wisdom was collected in our commencement speeches. Every year around this time, at podiums across America, people attempt to send our young adults off into the world with a bit of hard-won knowledge.

Presumably, that's what happened at both of my graduations. I don't recall. In high school, I'm pretty sure the speaker was a young woman who got good grades and who said something about achieving our dreams. My wife gave the commencement speech at her high school, but even she can't remember a thing she said.

At my college graduation, the speaker was a semi-famous writer who had penned a book about faith and the prairie. I assume she gave some sort of meditation on flatness, but all I remember is that her speech itself felt like driving across North Dakota.

This is the fate of so many people who sit on folding chairs, listening to a speaker trot out boilerplate platitudes and saccharine reassurances. It would have been nice to hear something useful. Something practical. Something worth remembering. Something like, "No matter what, always take the first parking spot you see." That would have saved me some time.

In his book *10½ Things No Commencement Speaker Has Ever Said*, the writer Charles Wheelan collects tidbits he wishes someone had told him. Things such as "Marry someone smarter than you."

He encourages graduates to take time off after college. When Wheelan told his mother that he and his girlfriend were going to backpack around the world, she protested that when he got back, he would be a year behind. "Behind what?" he wonders. "In nine months of traveling, I read more, I saw more, and I thought more than I did during any single year in college."

He also notes that "your parents don't want what's best for you," because often, what's best for you involves a degree of risk. Your parents want what's good for you. Another point: "Your time in fraternity basements was well spent." Wheelan doesn't think your time driving the porcelain bus was so wise. Rather, he notes that the root of the word fraternize is brotherhood, and that, according to one study, joining a group that meets every month may have the same effect on your sense of well-being as doubling your income.

That is something I wish I had known. My college speaker, who knew so much about prairies, should have mentioned that it's the people in your life who make all the difference. Make friends. Keep them. Beware of loneliness, because it is one of the most difficult and dangerous things you can face.

There are good commencement speeches. English teacher David McCullough Jr. made waves by telling students "You're not special" (something they were about to learn anyway), and lamenting that Americans have come to love accolades more than experience. A few years before that, author J.K. Rowling had some wise words about failure. "Rock bottom became the solid foundation on which I rebuilt my life," she observed. "You will never truly know yourself, or the strength of your relationships, until both have been tested by adversity."

What these sentiments have in common is the gritty honesty you seldom get. We would have remembered if someone had looked into our collective future and told us what was going to happen:

One of you will die trying to rescue a drowning child. One of you will go to jail. One of you will join a cult and cold-call the rest of you as recruits. One of you will drive your snowmobile into a tree. Some of you will achieve your dreams. Most of you will have to come up with something else. All of you will fail at something. If you're lucky, you will learn from this. In a few years, you will forget one another's names and faces. You will come to your reunion and meet people who are not the ones you knew, but versions of them — some better, some worse.

That might have gotten me thinking.

Wheelan advises graduates to read obituaries. "They remind us that interesting, successful people rarely lead orderly, linear lives," he writes. In a chapter called "It's All Borrowed Time," he tells the story of a brilliant friend who was a Rhodes scholar, a writer and activist, and who died before their 10th reunion. Another chapter is simply titled "I Have No Idea What the Future Will Bring."

In our most honest moments, we know this. We have no idea how we got where we are. None of us fully understands exactly how we succeeded, or why we failed. A lot of it is luck. What matters, though, isn't the luck itself, but what you do with it.

Maybe this is stuff you can learn only on your own. But I still would have liked to hear it: Your life will be a mess. And in the end, that's both the joy and the sorrow of it. That's what makes it mysterious. That's what makes it rewarding. That's what makes it terrifying. That's what makes it interesting. That's what makes it a life.

May 2013

The truth about fiction: On novels and business

For years, a giant paper brick sat on my shelf. Its spine read *The Count of Monte Cristo*. I avoided taking it down because I had other things to do. It clocked in at over a thousand pages of small print — almost half a million words. It hung like a millstone around the neck of my cultural conscience. It was one of the dreaded "classics" that I should have read long ago but never did.

This was easy to justify. After all, how could a nearly 200-year-old tale of intrigue set in revolutionary France relate to my world of computers and space tourism and YouTube cat videos?

Then one day I took the book off the shelf, started reading, and got hooked. Hours flew by. The world around me disappeared as the count and his elaborate web of plans came alive. Eventually, I would reemerge and fret over the time I'd wasted. I had deadlines to meet. I had bills to pay and a business to run. What could a made-up story have to do with that?

Everything, says cognitive psychologist Keith Oatley. "Business schools are realizing that being able to understand other people is important," he told me when I called him at his office in Toronto. "What we've found is that reading more fiction enables you to understand other people better. Fiction is about exploring a range of circumstances and interactions and characters you're likely to meet. Fiction is not a description of ordinary life; it's a simulation."

Oatley and his colleagues have performed several experiments that show how this works. In one study, they separated fiction readers from nonfiction readers and measured their social perceptiveness. The fiction group scored better at interpreting facial expressions and social cues. They also were less socially isolated and had more social support than nonfiction readers.

But do those who are already more socially adept read more fiction, or does fiction make them that way? Oatley's colleague Raymond Mar asked people to read either an essay or a short story from the *New Yorker*, then gave them all two tests — one social, one logical. Both groups did equally well on the logic test, but the fiction readers did better on the social one, suggesting that the fiction was improving their social acumen. As Oatley put it to me, "If you're going to fly a plane, you'd best spend some time in a flight simulator."

In 2005, professors Warren Bennis and James O'Toole lodged a complaint in the *Harvard Business Review* about the world of business education, which they said had become too enamored of the "scientific model."

"Though scientific research techniques may require considerable skill in statistics or experimental design," they wrote, "they call for little insight into complex social and human factors and minimal time in the field discovering the actual problems facing managers."

The two argued that business schools were leading people to become divorced from the real world, where they often must make decisions without all the facts. They also implied that this focus on the coldblooded, quantifiable side of business was one factor behind the scandals at Enron, WorldCom, and Arthur Andersen. A few years later, those scandals would look like dime-store thefts compared with the global meltdown. Bennis and O'Toole called on business schools to emulate Stanford professor James March, who taught a famous course on leadership using another door-stopping classic: *War and Peace*.

As Oatley writes: "History, [Aristotle] argued, tells us only what has happened, whereas fiction tells us what can happen, which can stretch our moral imaginations and give us insights into ourselves and other people."

By letting us see how people interact and by shoring up our ability to imagine what another person is thinking or feeling, fiction lets our brains try out new perspectives. Oatley has shown in his experiments that fiction "measurably enhances our abilities to empathize with other people and connect with something larger than ourselves."

It would be an oversimplification to say that having more fiction readers on Wall Street would have prevented the financial crisis. But in our technophilic era, it's worth thinking about. As Bennis and O'Toole wrote, "The problem is not that business schools have embraced scientific rigor, but that they have forsaken other forms of knowledge."

I finally did finish *The Count of Monte Cristo*. As I put it back in its place on the shelf, my eye drifted to other books. Hmm, I thought, *The Great Gatsby*. I remembered almost nothing about it from my high school reading. The book wasn't very long. I eyed the pile of work on my desk.

"Do I really have time to read this?" I asked myself. But maybe a better question is: "Do I have time not to?"

March 2013

The end of the world as we know it:
On ancient stories and distant futures

One morning as I was reading the paper, I came across an alarming headline: "A 'Code Red' on Climate Change." It went on: "New U.N. Report Shows Many Dire Effects Are Locked In; Avoiding Catastrophe Will Take Aggressive Action."

My daughter, who was 13, glanced over at it.

"I don't like how we're called Generation Z," she said. For a moment, I thought she was changing the subject.

"Really?" I asked her. "Why not?"

"Because it makes it seem like we're the last generation," she said. "Like we have to fix climate change and save the world. Or else we're the last generation. The one that fails."

"Well," I said nonchalantly, "the world isn't going to end in your lifetime."

"But what about my kids'?" she countered. "And my grandkids'?"

I hesitated: "… probably not then, either."

This wasn't exactly the reassurance she wanted, but the conversation had caught me off guard. Perhaps I should have been better prepared: Many parents have been seeing in their kids what's known as "eco-anxiety" or "climate anxiety" — a phenomenon that has become a major mental health issue for some children. Some adults have even experienced it themselves.

The recent publication of the first major study of eco-anxiety in young people across the globe has shed some light on the issue. Researchers from the University of Bath in England interviewed 10,000 people between the ages of 16 and 25 from countries including Finland, India, Nigeria, and the United States. Their findings were similar to the results of my own survey of one young person.

Across the world, 56 percent of young people feel that "humanity is doomed," while 75 percent agree that "the future is frightening." A whopping 84 percent are either extremely, very, or moderately worried about climate change — and 39 percent say they are hesitant to have children. The authors noted that "over 50 percent felt sad, anxious, angry, powerless, helpless, and guilty. More than 45 percent said their feelings about climate change negatively affected their daily life and functioning."

I don't think eco-anxiety has affected my daughter's ability to function, but it's clearly clouding her view of her future. And amid a constant drumbeat of dire predictions, with politicians announcing we only have something like 12 years left to fix climate change, it's no wonder.

For weeks afterward, I thought about this conversation. Often I found my mind going back to my own adolescent fears. As a young child, I was mildly traumatized by an episode of Pat Robertson's *700 Club* that showed evidence that the four horsemen of the apocalypse were on their way. In grade school in the 1980s, the threat that hung over us was nuclear war. In college, I worried about the "population bomb" that was set to go off any day. And then came Y2K, peak oil, the Mayan calendar, and so on.

Climate change may be fundamentally different from those other potential world-ending events. The science shows that climate change is happening and that humans are driving it. But humanity doesn't have a particularly great track record of predicting even the end of your average recession or pandemic, let alone the end of the world. And there are some good reasons to avoid end-times thinking and language.

"The problem with apocalypticism and this doom and gloom about our inevitable fate," says Sarah Jaquette Ray, author of *A Field Guide to Climate Anxiety: How to Keep Your Cool on a Warming Planet*, "is that most people psychologically either check out or give up. They become so despairing that it's hard for them to do the work that would be required to stave off that fate, or to adapt to it."

The emotional effects of climate apocalypticism are one reason to avoid that framing, especially with children. "Telling kids over and over that their fate is sealed by what happens in the next 10 years is not only not true," Ray says, "it's cruel. It's unethical."

Another reason to not use doomsday language is that it isn't solely a reflection of the climate situation — it's also a reflection of what's known as the negativity bias, in which humans tend to give more weight to negative information than to positive.

"Urgency and apocalypse sell," Ray says. "It's really effective. On the political side, it gets people to surrender stuff. It helps pass legislation. But the doom and gloom is not necessarily the only reality we live in. The science is nuanced. There's so much gray area, but there's enough evidence that many things are improving, or turning around, or people are taking action, that we must hold on to that to counterbalance the negativity bias in the news and in our brains."

Michael Shellenberger, author of *Apocalypse Never: Why Environmental Alarmism Hurts Us All*, contrasts what he calls "apocalyptic environmentalism" with "environmental humanism," which he defines as an approach that puts economic development and technology at the center of the environmental effort.

In his book, he points out that many of the things we take to be signs of the end of the world are actually more complex than they might seem. And, he notes, there are positive trends that don't make the headlines. "U.S. carbon emissions declined 22 percent between 2005 and 2020," Shellenberger says. "That's massive. The Paris Agreement called for 17 percent. So we beat the target, which never happens."

While some of that decline was due to the pandemic, it accelerated a trend that was already underway. And it gets us closer to where we need to be.

"The risk of triggering tipping points increases at higher planetary temperatures," Shellenberger writes, "and thus our goal should be to reduce emissions and keep temperatures as low as possible without undermining economic development."

Even though the climate situation may be starting to turn around, the appeal of the apocalyptic scenario still runs deep. Shellenberger points out how climate apocalypticism mirrors some of the myths in the Judeo-Christian tradition. But in truth, it may go back even further.

In his book *The Origins of the World's Mythologies*, Michael Witzel, a professor of Sanskrit at Harvard, looked at myths from across the world and mapped the similarities. What he found was that mythologies from across the globe share a certain structure, or narrative: one in which the world is created in darkness or chaos, then goes through various ages until, finally, it ends.

Tracing these stories through time and geography, Witzel found that the original narrative probably emerged somewhere in southwestern Asia about 40,000 years ago, then spread with human migration across emerging cultures, appearing as far away as Iceland and the Inca empire.

All of these cultures' mythologies share what Witzel calls the "Laurasian" storyline — named for Laurasia, the ancient northern landmass on whose remnants many of these mythologies evolved. Over time, it proved remarkably powerful and subsumed nearly all other mythological systems. All major world religions are founded on a Laurasian narrative, where the world is born in a cosmic soup and ends in a bang, and today 95 percent of the world's people subscribe to some version of it.

None of this, of course, is very helpful to your average 13-year-old kid. But the realization that for as long as 40,000 years we have been predicting the end of the world, and it has yet to arrive, could provide some stress relief. Maybe for now it's enough to assume that the future will probably not look much like our predictions. Because the apocalyptic narrative and the resulting climate anxiety can ruin your day, and even your life. And it could become a self-fulfilling prophecy that destroys our world.

"It requires work to focus on the positive," Ray says. "It's very hard. It's a discipline. But we have all the technology we need to do this. We have all the science we need to do this. We have significant political and public will. We're poised to do some important stuff here."

For my part, I'll tell my daughter that climate change is a problem to be solved and that we are on our way to solving it. I will tell her that hope is humanity's greatest renewable resource. And I will tell her that good things are happening, and that they matter at least as much as the bad.

December 2021

ROTARY

Meeting like this: On meetings and mundanity

Imagine, if you will, the worst meeting of your life: The clock moves more slowly than the laws of physics should allow. Garbled strands of jargon fall from the mouths of those around you. Whatever vague goals had been uttered before the meeting are forgotten, left far behind, like roadkill on a long ride to nowhere.

That trapped feeling is probably as old as the first tribal gathering. And judging by some books for sale today (*Meetings Suck*, *Death by Meeting*), not much has changed in the intervening millennia.

Meetings may be one of the most maligned and dreaded of humanity's rituals, but they are not going away. Nor should they: Every week, some 1.2 million Rotarians meet around the world in an effort to make it a little better. Every year, meetings, conferences, and conventions across the United States inject around $280 billion into the economy. And every day, millions of people meet at their workplace to try to move their company toward some goal.

Clearly there is some reason we keep on meeting like this. Why haven't Skype, FaceTime, and other technologies made face-to-face meetings obsolete?

As a writer, I always find meeting in person far more informative than talking to people on the phone. It has a value that's hard to quantify. One study did show that groups who met face to face came up with a larger number of creative ideas, with more variety and quality, than those who met via video or voice.

Then why do we feel so tortured, so shackled by meetings? Why do they often feel so pointless?

These days, I attend a lot of meetings, but they are mostly small and purposeful and of my own design. But in college, I belonged to several campus groups whose main purpose seemed to be not getting things done. When I was an English teacher in Tanzania, our school's staff meetings lasted several hours; any religious gathering lasted much longer.

During such meetings, I sometimes entered a trancelike state — a bureaucratic stupor — that passed for attention and preserved my sanity. Occasionally, though, it did backfire. At our school's graduation, I heard my name from a distance, then realized I was being called upon to stand up and say in Swahili, "Praise the Lord." In my daze, what I said was, "The Lord has gone away on a journey."

Many of us share this ambivalence about meetings: On the one hand, they are essential. On the other, they are essentially a waste of time. Al Pittampalli, author of *Read This Before Our Next Meeting: How We Can Get More Done*, says there's a reason for this. Pittampalli is a former executive at Ernst & Young, where he became so frustrated by how little was accomplished in endless staff meetings, standing meetings, and status meetings that he decided to try to unravel the problem.

"I found myself sitting in a lot of bad meetings," Pittampalli recalled when I phoned him. "I couldn't quite understand why so much of our time seemed to be wasted. When I voiced this to people, they seemed to feel it was the cost of doing business. But I refused to accept that." Pittampalli's research led him to a counterintuitive conclusion: Most meetings are designed to waste time.

"The meetings I would attend lacked any kind of clear purpose," he says. "It took me a long time to figure out that this was intentional. This lack of an outcome to meetings is not a bug, it's a feature. It allows us to escape the hard work of making decisions, which is essentially what the whole meeting problem is all about."

We hold meetings because we know we should consult our coworkers before making decisions. Making decisions is hard, and decisions have consequences. So we hold meetings to postpone decisions, rather than to make them. We call a meeting to discuss a new marketing campaign rather than to decide to launch that campaign. If we did the latter, it would be a clear outcome. We would know whether the meeting had been successful.

This is why, by one estimate, half the time spent in the 11 million meetings held in the United States every day is wasted, and why workers are said to "lose" an average of four workdays a month to meetings.

So meetings are a waste of time.

Actually, Pittampalli says no — in fact, they are quite the opposite. "I'm all for the idea of in-person debates and conversations," he says. "We're designed to reason with each other in person. There's this great feedback loop that happens when you talk something out. You say something and the other person interprets it and responds verbally or nonverbally, and you get this really rapid exchange that can help you get to good ideas quickly."

Certainly, many meetings are destined to fail. Even when goals are set out clearly, it doesn't mean those goals will be met or that those decisions will be made. And there are other reasons your meetings can get stuck in productive purgatory.

Someone in the group, for instance, may be heeding the advice of a pamphlet called the "Simple Sabotage Field Manual." This handbook, put out in 1944 by the U.S. Office of Strategic Services (a precursor to the CIA), suggested ways ordinary citizens could sabotage a hostile power. Under the section "General Interference with Organizations and Production," the OSS identified techniques for bogging down organizations — including "Insist on doing everything through 'channels,'" "Talk as frequently as possible and at great length," "Illustrate your 'points' by long anecdotes and accounts of personal experiences," and "Bring up irrelevant issues as frequently as possible."

Sound familiar?

If you are concerned about workplace saboteurs, you can consult the 2015 book *Simple Sabotage: A Modern Field Manual for Detecting and Rooting Out Everyday Behaviors That Undermine Your Workplace*. Many of those unhelpful behaviors start out as good things — trying to get input and follow procedures. But when they are seen as ends in themselves, they start to bog things down. Recognizing (and calling out) this kind of sabotage is a first step. Beyond that, keep expectations clear, don't let fear of risks and failure guide you, and set deadlines for committees to complete their work. (Also: Never, ever cc everyone on an email.)

Other times, however, it is not the sabotage that is simple, but the group itself. There is a metric known as collective intelligence, which is the ability of a small group to function well and to complete the tasks set before it. Researchers have found that a group's collective intelligence bears no relation to the average or maximum intelligence of its members.

Rather, it's related to those members' social sensitivity. The study, published in *Science*, found that groups with more women were more collectively intelligent and that "groups where a few people dominated the conversation were less collectively intelligent than those with a more equal distribution of conversational turn-taking."

So even if you're the smartest one at the meeting, wait your turn. If you try to ram your brilliance down other people's throats, you'll make the whole group dumber.

Most of us are familiar with this dynamic in mundane, everyday meetings. But it can also be a problem in critically important meetings such as peace talks, says Daniel Shapiro, a professor of psychology at Harvard University and the author of *Negotiating the Nonnegotiable: How to Resolve Your Most Emotionally Charged Conflicts*.

"The term 'peace talks' can be deceptive, because the most important part of the talks is listening," he told me. "The reason peace talks fail is that everyone talks and no one listens. And if people don't feel heard, they'll say, 'You don't know us. You don't know our pain.' Once those at the table feel their stories truly have been heard, you can begin to move forward."

The stakes of most of our meetings are not nearly as high as peace in the Middle East. But lessons can still be learned from those meetings. Shapiro advocates thinking through what he calls "the four P's" before any meeting starts. *Purpose*: What are we trying to achieve? *Process*: How is this meeting going to function? *People*: Who should be there? And *Product*: What needs to happen by the end of the meeting?

He also cautions those in emotionally charged meetings to avoid what he calls "vertigo," in which they get so consumed by a conflict that they can't think beyond it. But in the end, sitting across from the other side is the only way everyone can move forward together. "When you're building something as fragile as peace," Shapiro says, "nothing beats human interaction."

That's something every Rotarian knows well.

September 2017

Hit the mark: On help and humility

There are many slums around Nairobi. The people living in them don't have access to many of the things we have. It would be nice to help them.

That was the thought behind a project carried out by one U.S. Rotary club from a "very friendly district," according to Geeta Manek, governor of District 9200, which includes Kenya. Some members of the club had volunteered at a community center in the Mukuru slums. They found that the slums had no toilets or showers, and they wanted to fix that. So they made a grant of $2,000 available to build two of each.

Some time later, one of the club members traveled to Kenya and decided to check on the project. The toilets and showers had no handles and were sitting unused. Manek got an exasperated call and was asked to go check it out. "The knobs were not on because there was no money for connecting the water from the main line," Manek says, "and there was no place to get rid of the used water. The knobs would have been stolen. So we had to come up with extra money to supply water and to put a caretaker there. The problem was that a feasibility study was not done. Nobody had gone and checked out, What are we going to do before and after the project?"

This is not an uncommon phenomenon, says Ted Rose, a California native who has lived in Colima, Mexico, for 28 years. A member of the Rotary Club of Colima, he frequently speaks to clubs and districts about how to avert such problems. "I've been a Rotary volunteer around the world and helped a lot of clubs be successful with grants. In the process, I've made every possible mistake a guy can make," he says. "I've also seen a lot of other people's mistakes."

He cites an incident that arose when a young woman, the daughter of a California Rotarian, volunteered at an orphanage in Guatemala. After she came home, her father's club decided to build the orphanage a carpentry workshop so the children could learn a valuable trade. A good idea — in theory. But after four years (and thousands of dollars), some of the Rotarians went to see the project and found that the tools had been stolen and the shop was standing empty. The children at the orphanage could not remember it ever having been used. What went wrong? Something simple: No one had asked the orphanage if it needed, or wanted, a carpentry shop. Rose says this lack of support from recipients is one of the main reasons projects fail.

The realization that these conversations must happen may seem an obvious one, but it has been long in coming. It is also part of a larger trend in thinking about assistance and aid. The last few years have seen a debate over whether aid itself is even a good idea. Economists Dambisa Moyo, author of *Dead Aid: Why Aid Is Not Working and How There Is a Better Way for Africa*, and William Easterly, author of *The White Man's Burden: Why the West's Efforts to Aid the Rest Have Done So Much Ill and So Little Good*, say that the trillion or so dollars poured into Africa since 1960 have not been effective. Each year, the continent loses about $148 billion (about 25 percent of the GDP of African states) to corruption, yet some African countries get more than half their budgets from aid. To what end?

There is a big difference between large-scale aid and the smaller projects of individual Rotary clubs. But the change in thinking is relevant to both. In the past, people thought poverty was a simple lack of money or things. Fixing it meant adding money and things. But it's not that easy.

Economists such as Harvard's Michael Kremer are calling for "smart aid," which targets specific issues and rigorously measures results. Other people, such as Emeka Okafor, a blogger and entrepreneur who launched the One Million African Lives Initiative in 2006, have pushed for aid that bypasses government coffers and instead invests in civil society and social institutions.

The terminology these days is about investment, trade, growth, results, and accountability. Even Bono and Bob Geldof have started investment funds. The "appropriate technology" movement, which once held that supplying people with the right machines was all that was needed for development, has given way to a market-driven approach led by Paul Polak and the "social entrepreneurs" who look for unmet demands, then create products to sell. They help people, make money, and everyone feels some ownership over the result.

All these changes boil down to one thing: asking people what they need instead of telling them. It means treating them like partners. It also reflects a shift of focus from alleviating poverty as an abstract idea to the messy reality of helping people who don't have much money. Unless you know a certain part of the world intimately, the chances of you knowing how to solve its problems are small. The solution? Ask. Investigate. Repeat.

Change is happening on both ends. District 9200 is a Future Vision pilot district. Kaushik Manek, Geeta Manek's husband and also a past district governor, says that all projects now must include a feasibility study and will be examined by auditing and monitoring teams. "We want sustainable projects, not handouts," he says. A little further south, in Arusha, Tanzania, another past district governor, Amir Somji, noted that because Arusha is a tourist city, Rotarians there see a lot of dubious project proposals.

"People come here to travel, and they see poverty," Somji says. "Fair enough. But it is a bad project when they say, 'Please help this village there.' Then it is not our choice. It's the choice of people from outside. You don't want the project to be thrust upon you. You want a project that you are also passionate about."

Rose lists several qualities that help projects succeed: Training and education, because if people don't understand the project, it's much more likely to fail. Maintenance. And local knowledge, whether that means working with an area Rotary club or another organization with a long track record there. "That way if any bad stuff was going to show up, it would have already shown up," he says. "One of the projects I work on in Mexico has been there for 27 years." Rotary International conventions and project fairs are good places to find host partners.

But the most important aspects are the ownership, the partnership, and the communication. To achieve those, approach with more questions than answers. Ask the people what their community needs. Then ask what they think is the best way to meet that need. And then ask if that's what the project will accomplish. Beginning with that attitude is the best way to ensure the effort will serve the greatest number of people for as long as possible.

October 2012

Lowering the temperature: On peace and conflict

Jean Best was about to resign from Rotary. It was a sad day for her: She loved being a Rotarian. But she had become enmeshed in a conflict with another member of her club. Although she tried to engage with that member to defuse the situation, the problem persisted. Best could have pressed the issue, could have tried to run it all the way up the flagpole. But instead, she decided to back away. She left that club and joined the Rotary Club of Newton Stewart, Scotland, where she's very happy. But she hasn't given up on addressing the larger issue: "Now I'm looking at conflict resolution in Rotary clubs," she says.

Conflict resolution is something we humans have been trying to master at least since the first Cro-Magnon tribal steering committee. Some scientists who study the fossil record say that for much of history, people have dealt with conflict through violence. Some even theorize that our very ability to work as a team evolved out of our need to compete against other groups.

And while bench-clearing brawls may be rare at your Rotary club, that doesn't mean your meetings always end in a chorus of "Kumbaya" — especially at a moment in history when the fractiousness of the world seems to seep into our lives in unexpected ways. "The conflict in clubs is growing," says Jo Pawley, 2019-20 governor of District 1020 (Scotland). "I've seen examples of bullying. I've seen people being downright rude. I've seen examples of people not leaving things alone, pulling the scab off something you think has been resolved."

Calum Thomson, Pawley's successor as district governor, agrees. "Every club's got issues. They might be minor, minuscule, not that fundamental. But we've all got issues," he says.

"It's difficult to talk about conflict in clubs because many Rotarians don't realize that there is conflict in clubs," Best says. "So it's about raising awareness to begin with about what a modern, 21st-century Rotary is all about. If we want Rotary to continue as the great organization it is, we need to start changing the way we conduct our Rotary club meetings. It's about clubs putting greater emphasis on how they discuss issues, rather than what they discuss. We found that people were leaving clubs because they were not listened to or were not spoken to appropriately. Talking and listening should be an important part of Rotary. Into this comes an awareness of bias, diversity, and stereotypes."

Rotary clubs aren't the only place where conflict occurs, of course. We live in an age of rage: road rage, air rage, office rage, bike rage, quarantine rage. Online, we're subjected to Twitter fights, Facebook unfriendings, Nextdoor knockdowns, and LinkedIn lashings.

An entire field of study is dedicated to systematically learning how to ratchet down disagreements, cool emotions, and help everyone be happy with getting less than they wanted. Conflict resolution isn't something that was invented recently.

It's also not the exclusive province of Western diplomats and academics. The European Union is a well-known "peace system," but there's also the Iroquois Great League of Peace and Power in New York, the tribes of the Upper Xingu River basin in Brazil, and the aboriginal tribes of the Western Desert in Australia. According to one study of what they all have in common, the impetus behind these systems was to manage conflict between neighboring societies before it rose to the level of war. Some employ what's known as an active peace system, while others rely on passive systems that use avoidance and toleration.

But how can we use the active system to address interpersonal conflicts, not just societal ones? Best has developed a four-seminar program to help keep meetings, Rotary club meetings included, moving along smoothly and openly. "One of the watchwords we use is, 'Get curious before you get furious,'" she says. "In other words, ask, 'Why did you say that? Why did you do that?' before you get angry. In a lot of cases, people just fly off the handle and walk out the door. It's about saying, 'Hang on a minute, let's discuss this. Let's open this up. Tell me why you feel like this. What have I said that's upset you?' It's a way of defusing the situation."

In 2020, Thomson and Pawley started working with Best to help train their district's incoming club presidents in conflict resolution. "It's all about listening to people," says Thomson. "And when they say something, you need to be able to repeat it back to them. So you're saying, 'I think this is what you said,' so there are no misunderstandings and we both know what we're talking about."

"Jean has this brilliant test where you have to describe something but you can't use nouns," says Pawley. The test consists of two people sitting back to back, so neither one can see the other. One person has to draw what the other person is describing. "What tends to happen is that you draw something completely not what was being described," she says. "It shows you that your listening skills are not as good as you think they are. It shows that you have to listen more to what is actually being said." The exercise also shows the speakers how their words can be misinterpreted, so everyone involved learns how communication can go wrong.

Best, who worked in education for nearly 40 years as a teacher, a head teacher, and finally as an inspector of schools for the Scottish government, makes this point too. "People, especially older people, in Rotary think they know how to talk to each other," she says, "but they actually don't. They think they're listening, and they're not. And we prove to them that they don't know how to talk and that they don't know how to listen."

Louisa Weinstein, a mediator who wrote a guide called "The 7 Principles of Conflict Resolution: How to Resolve Disputes, Defuse Difficult Situations and Reach Agreement," agrees with this approach. "The first, basic thing is to listen — to really listen, as a mirror to the other person," she says. "I might reflect back what the other person has said, and it might be absolutely to the letter what they said. And they may still come back to me and say, 'No, no. I didn't say that.'"

This happens because often we say things that we don't mean or mean things that we don't say. But an even bigger obstacle is that we all think we're right. "We need to assume a nonjudgmental attitude," says Weinstein. "If I'm going to resolve conflict, I need to be open to the fact that my judgment may not be valid, even if I think I'm absolutely right. Besides, being right isn't necessarily going to help anyway. It's about trying to understand, rather than to be understood."

In Best's system, once a conflict is out in the open, all parties offer ideas for resolution, which are discussed and considered. Finally, the person who has the conflict chooses the first step forward, followed by the others. This gives each party more ownership over the outcome.

As Best herself knows, this doesn't always work. Still, it's far better than just hoping a conflict will quietly disappear. Arguments within clubs, she says, have resulted in more than a few members dropping out. "Quite often it's because of something that's been said, or someone hasn't been listened to properly and then there's no discussion," she says.

"We can't afford to do this. Rotary is too important to the world to lose Rotarians over silly disagreements."

February 2021

Beyond borders: On youth exchange

Mara Egherman, a college librarian, was sitting at her desk when she saw an email pop up: Ryan Ahmad, a Muslim exchange student in Iowa from the Philippines, needed a place to stay. There had been trouble at his school, and he'd been beaten up by a fellow exchange student.

Egherman flashed back to her 16-year-old self, alone in a foreign country. "I knew I had to take this kid in," she says.

As a high school student, Egherman had applied for an exchange program in South Africa. But after arriving in Johannesburg in 1982, she discovered that her host family had racial notions that dovetailed with those of the apartheid regime. Egherman was forbidden from speaking to the help. The family considered Nelson Mandela (then still in prison) a terrorist. And they kept a cache of weapons in a closet for protection. For a teenager from the Midwest, this was disorienting — and eye-opening. Egherman saw people being treated in ways she'd never imagined.

Yet at school, she made lifelong friends, one of whom invited her home for the last few months of her exchange. Egherman's new family couldn't have been more different, with three sisters and lots of laughter. Because that friend reached out to Egherman, her exchange experience was a positive one. She came home a changed person, with an enhanced ability to imagine the lives of people in other places. That was the whole reason she'd signed up to go abroad.

Most exchange programs have one goal in mind: to expose young people to other cultures in order to promote international understanding and peace. The thought is that it's harder to hate someone you know. Scientists call this the contact hypothesis, and it's the idea behind not only Rotary Youth Exchange — which European clubs started in the 1920s, and which sends roughly 8,000 students to about 80 countries each year — but also programs such as Seeds of Peace and the post-9/11 Kennedy-Lugar Youth Exchange and Study Program, which brought Ahmad to Iowa in 2012.

When Rotary Youth Exchange began, the bitter, bloody memories of World War I were still fresh. It was part of a larger movement that hoped to increase ties between cultures and nations — and that picked up momentum after World War II.

The effort to temper nationalism, sectarianism, and tribalism also included the founding of the United Nations, the adoption of the Universal Declaration of Human Rights, the undertaking of the Nuremberg trials, and the success of the American civil rights movement.

Historically, groups have tended to regard themselves as operating at a higher level — as being better, more human — than the people around them. According to Samuel Bowles of the Santa Fe Institute and Jung-Kyoo Choi at Kyungpook National University in Korea, the tendency to be altruistic toward those who are members of our in-group and callous toward those who are not gave us an advantage over other hominids. They call it "parochial altruism," an evolutionary strategy not unlike that of the dreaded Argentine ant, which has colonized huge swaths of the planet. These ants refuse to fight one another, and separate colonies sometimes team up. Yet they are extremely aggressive toward other species of ants. The group grows stronger in uniting against the others. If Bowles and Choi are right, then evolution equipped us with an ability to draw a line between us and them, to separate the in-group from the out-group, to shut off our capacity to see through others' eyes.

Fortunately, there is a key difference in this respect between humans and ants: As we cross the lines between groups and see how thin they really are, our definition of "us" — of who's in our circle — can change.

That is what Egherman and other exchange students have experienced. So when she got the email about Ahmad, she knew she had a debt to pay. She understood what a difference she could make for this kid — lonely, in trouble, and far from home. A few days after she responded, Ahmad showed up at her family's door in Des Moines. Their house was next to a university, their neighborhood full of immigrants from Africa, Vietnam, and Mexico. At Ahmad's new school, he thrived immediately.

"Within three hours of being at our house, he had friends," Egherman recalls. He spent time with her 15-year-old daughter and her 10-year-old son. He hung out at the local mall and went to his new classmates' homes for dinner. And by the end of the year, he didn't want to leave.

As Egherman watched him blossom, she hoped she'd passed along the same gift she'd received all those years ago. She hoped she'd done everything she could — for him, for her, and for all of us — to make the circle a little bigger than it was before.

September 2014

Off the cuff: On public speaking

When I was in high school, public speaking was not considered glamorous. It was a required course relished only by people who also approached debate as a sport or who were thrilled by the prospect of student government.

The rest of us dutifully stood at the front of the class, reading rushed words off index cards, trying to picture our classmates in their underwear, but feeling naked instead. When it was over, we were glad we would never have to do that again.

Life, however, has a funny way of making you regret much of what you did — and didn't do — in high school. Some years later, as a writer, I found myself giving readings and talks. I realized I would actually have to know how to stand up in front of (fully clothed) people and give a speech.

Being a decent writer doesn't make you a decent speaker, and I quickly discovered that public speaking wasn't something I could wing. As my high school teacher tried to tell us, it's a skill that must be acquired.

I started looking around for help and found an organization formed by people in my shoes. We met weekly. Everybody stood up and spoke. We had to give a succession of speeches, which was hard at first. I gave a speech introducing myself, then went on to give others about things like Googling myself and the Dunning-Kruger effect. (Look it up.) People laughed and seemed to enjoy them, so I relaxed and gradually improved.

What was worse was the part of the meeting when one person stood up and selected victims at random for questions on a given topic. When chosen, we had to speak for two minutes without stopping. It was timed, and it was terrifying. My mind would go blank. My sense of humor vanished. I would sit like an arctic hare trying to blend in with my surroundings. One time I talked for a minute, then froze. The next minute was filled with nothing but silence.

Fortunately, the group was a forgiving one — they had all been there. And even this exercise became more bearable as my symptoms of public speaking anxiety (Mark Twain was the first to call it "stage fright") became less severe. Glossophobia is a common phenomenon, especially for those of us who are introverts, but it's an irony of our era that, despite all the ways we can communicate virtually, we want more than ever to hear from speakers directly.

For a fee, companies like Oratory Laboratory and Vow Muse will write toasts, personal speeches, even wedding vows for you. Websites offer to help with public speaking anxiety. You can even send your kid to public speaking summer camp. Because sooner or later, we know we'll all have to get up and say something. "The demand is increasing," says speaking coach Jezra Kaye, who works with business executives. "More people are expected to use public speaking skills at work. And many people are now aware of a public speaking career, because of things like TED Talks."

TED Talks, which mix storytelling and social science, have bestowed a strange new celebrity on people who previously would have kept their noses in books. They rack up millions of views online. They launch careers. They have become so successful, such a cultural force, that they have even inspired a backlash: Critics call them a glorified self-help forum or "middlebrow megachurch infotainment." Either way, TED Talks have made public speaking sexy. But as fun and informative as they can be, it's best to watch them with an impartial eye.

"What I would love for people to understand," says Kaye, "is that it doesn't make sense to compare yourself to what you see when you're watching a national TED Talk. When you're looking at TED.com, it's important to understand you're looking at the end result of hundreds of hours of guided preparation. You're looking at a video that was edited from a four-camera shoot. You're looking at somebody's job for the year before they give that talk."

While inspiring, TED Talks shouldn't be the yardstick by which we measure our own speeches. But one thing we should take from them is the realization that storytelling, if done right, can make every speech better.

"Stories need a lot of work," says Kaye. "They have to be shaped, and they have to be shaped by trial and error. You don't know what the audience is going to respond to until you tell the story — particularly if it's a funny story." She recommends practicing a story out loud, in front of people, at least a dozen times before taking it on stage.

It's too late for me to go back to high school, but I did want more instruction. So I went to the library and found an audio course called "The Art of Public Speaking," by an archaeologist named John Hale. He uses some of the great speeches in history — by Gandhi, Queen Elizabeth, Marie Curie, Tecumseh, and Demosthenes of Athens, among others — to illustrate how to be a better speaker.

The tips were pretty basic: Use humor. Be yourself. Practice, practice, practice. Those were probably the same techniques our teachers gave us all those years ago. But hearing the words, and in some cases the actual voices, of the people who put those words to use was brilliant. It reminded me that even before the internet, PowerPoints, and TED Talks, public speaking — oratory — has always been a force in human affairs.

Speeches have launched wars. They have changed the course of history. Hale quotes one of the greatest orators of modern times, Winston Churchill: "Of all the talents bestowed upon men, none is so precious as the gift of oratory. He who enjoys it wields a power more durable than that of a great king."

So this growing hunger to hear things directly from people is not surprising. The spoken word, whether used to close a sale or open a mind, remains one of the most powerful forces in the world.

December 2015

The vindication of vaccination: On medicine and truth

Not long after our first daughter was born, I remember seeing her on the exam table in the doctor's office, lying on her back, with the white paper crinkling underneath her. She was soft and small and fragile. I remember watching the needle pierce her leg, and feeling a strange mix of guilt and relief. There was a slight delay before her face changed and her scream filled the room. As a father, I cringed.

In 2006, there were rumors about mercury in the injections, and some possible link with autism. My wife and I had heard them. With the anxiety of all new parents, we wanted, more than anything, to keep our daughter from harm. But sorting through the opinions and anecdotes and research was overwhelming. We were torn between fear, belief, and trust.

Fortunately, we had a good doctor whom we did trust, who assured us that the shots didn't contain mercury and that they posed no risk of autism. We believed her. We were too exhausted to do much more than that. Things might have been harder if we'd felt differently about our doctor, or about Western medicine, or about the world. But we didn't. We just did our best. Today our daughter is healthy and thriving. For that we're grateful. Yet a surprising number of new parents in my generation don't feel the way we did. They don't believe their doctors. And they haven't come to see vaccinations as an obvious, logical, low-risk choice.

Part of this reluctance initially stemmed from a paper published in the medical journal *The Lancet* in 1998, which implied that the measles-mumpsrubella vaccine caused autism and bowel disease. The study was small, with only 12 subjects, and its results were never reproduced. *The Lancet* eventually retracted it. And the paper's lead author, Andrew Wakefield, was found to have committed deliberate fraud and was barred from practicing medicine in the United Kingdom. But it was too late: A movement had started, headed by parents (some of them celebrities) who were, most of all, afraid.

Today, much more is known. There is no detectable link between vaccines and autism. Yet no matter how many studies come to this conclusion, it doesn't seem to matter. The anti-vaccine campaign tapped into a deep anxiety about science, the world, and our place within it. Resistance to vaccination is not a new thing: Anti-vaccination movements gained momentum in Britain in the early 1800s almost as soon as the practice was established. A backlash arose on this side of the Atlantic as well, with the formation of the Anti-Vaccination Society of America and the Anti-Vaccination League of New York City in the late 1800s. Some people simply didn't believe vaccination worked. Some feared it caused eczema. Others felt it was un-Christian.

The word *inoculate* originally meant "to graft" or "implant," from the Latin *oculus*, meaning "eye" or "bud." But to many, the idea of vaccination — infecting one's body with a sickness in order to prevent that sickness — seemed counterintuitive. And planting the "bud" from which immunity would grow frequently meant accepting a measure of risk and pain for a greater good.

The zeitgeist these days is often the opposite: to insulate, a word that comes from the Latin for "island." That's what many parents dream of creating when they opt not to vaccinate: an island where their child is safe from harm.

Yet by forgoing vaccinations, they are creating a different kind of island. In the wealthy school districts of Los Angeles, according to an investigation by the *Hollywood Reporter*, as many as 60 to 70 percent of parents have filed "personal belief exemptions" so they won't be required to vaccinate their children. The rate of vaccination in those schools is comparable to that of Chad and South Sudan. And long-forgotten diseases such as measles are reemerging.

Many anti-vaccination advocates argue that immunization is a personal choice that affects only them. But this decision affects our entire society. This is because of a phenomenon called "herd immunity," which means that each additional person who is vaccinated decreases the ability of a virus to spread. At a certain threshold, the virus can't find enough hosts to move through a population. In the best case, it goes extinct. That's what happened with smallpox, and that's what Rotary is working toward with the polio eradication campaign. Without vaccination, many people can contract a disease — sometimes without showing any symptoms — and then carry it to others who cannot be vaccinated because they are too young or too ill.

Eula Biss is an essayist who had a son in the early 2000s and heard the same sort of rumors my wife and I did. She did some deep research before coming down on the side of vaccination. But she remained fascinated by the cultural currents stirred up by the topic, and her investigations resulted in her book *On Immunity: An Inoculation*. In it, she notes: "Immunity is a public space. And it can be occupied by those who choose not to carry immunity." The ultimate effect is to endanger the most vulnerable members of society.

Past waves of anti-vaccine movements flourished when little was known about viruses and how they spread. And while today's movement has some aspects in common with its predecessors, Biss feels there is something different about it too — namely that it stems from a sense of powerlessness in the face of unseen toxins and pollutants and evils.

"What has been done to us," she writes, "is that we have been made fearful. What will we do with our fear? This strikes me as a central question of both citizenship and motherhood. As mothers, we must somehow square our power with our powerlessness. We can protect our children to some extent. But we cannot make them invulnerable any more than we can make ourselves invulnerable."

But if we have gained some fears, we have lost others. It's been a long time since we dealt with the reality of measles or rubella or smallpox. It's been a long time since we lived as hunter-gatherers whose child mortality rate was 100 times the one we currently enjoy in the United States. It's been a long time since we couldn't just assume our child would live.

Perhaps it's time to bring vaccination back from the personal into the public sphere. To ask who we are vaccinating for: For the young. For the old. For those weaker than ourselves. For those in future generations. For everyone.

When the question is framed this way, researchers find that people are more likely to choose vaccination. And this is as it should be, because vaccination is not a personal decision, such as what we want to eat or what we want to wear. Vaccination is not a lifestyle choice. Vaccination is not simply an individual matter. Because no matter what kind of island we feel we are on, we are on it together.

April 2015

Acknowledgements

This book would not have been possible without the encouragement and steady hand of Jenny Llakmani, my editor at *Rotary* who was willing to entertain some wild ideas and shepherd them into legible prose. Thank you, Jenny, for letting me run.

A huge thanks also to the other Rotary magazine editors and staff I worked with on these essay over the years, Including John Rezak, Hank Sartin, Diana Shoenberg, Geoff Johnson, Cynthia Edbroke Jason Keyser and others. It's one of the best crews I've worked with. Thanks also to Doug Mack for help with the cover of this book.

I also want to thank the many scientists and researchers who took time out of their busy schedules to try to answer the questions at the core of these essays, questions like: Can believing old age is decline cause you to age faster? What is the value of a photograph in the age of infinite photographs? How exactly does living in another culture make you more creative? And many more

Thanks to all the Rotarians across the world who have welcomed me into their clubs, and who have given their time and attention to these essays in the magazine, and for making a space like Rotary magazine, where stories of hope can find an audience of people willing to work on solving problems.

Thanks also to my daughters, Libby and Josie, who gave me permission to use their words in these pages more than once. They are funnier and more thoughtful than I was at their age—or any age.

And thanks most of all to my wife and life partner, Bridgit. As the wife of a writer, she finds herself as a character more than she would probably like, but is always gracious about it. Thank you for steering me away from the lonely path of my aspirations. I would much rather be with you than be Gandhi.

The Author

Frank Bures is author of *The Geography of Madness*, a book about "cultural syndromes" that *Newsweek* called one of the best travel books of the decade. His work has been included in *The Best American Travel Writing*, selected as "Notable" in *The Best American Essays* and *Best American Sports Writing*, and has appeared in *Harper's, The Atlantic, The Washington Post Magazine,* along with other publications. He has lived in Italy, Tanzania, New Zealand, Thailand, and other places, and he now resides in in Minneapolis with his wife, Bridgit, and two daughters. You can find more of his work at frankbures.com.

The essays in this collection were originally published in *Rotary* magazine between 2010 and 2021. Among other accolades, "What Price Experience?" was selected as "Notable" in *The Best American Essays 2015*; "Beyond Belief" was selected as "Notable" in *The Best American Essays 2016*; and "Meeting Like This" won Folio Magazine's Eddie & Ozzie Award in 2018 for Best Association/Nonprofit Column.